EXPLORING

THE WORLD OF PHYSICS

From Simple Machines To Nuclear Energy

JOHN HUDSON TINER

EXPLORING
THE WORLD OF PHYSICS

First printing: May 2006

Fourth printing: October 2013

Copyright © 2006 by John Hudson Tiner. All rights reserved. No part of this book may be used or reproduced in any manner whatsoever without written permission of the publisher except in the case of brief quotations in articles and reviews. For information write:

Master Books, P.O. Box 726, Green Forest, AR 72638.

Master Books® is a division of the New Leaf Publishing Group, Inc.

ISBN-13: 978-0-89051-466-5

Library of Congress Catalog Number: 2005936557

Interior Design and Layout: Carol and Eric Sawyer of Rose Design, Greenfield Center, NY 12833

Please consider requesting that a copy of this volume be purchased by your local library system.

Printed in the United States of America

Please visit our website for other great titles:

www.masterbooks.net

For information regarding author interviews, please contact the publicity department at (870) 438-5288.

Dedication

This book is dedicated to Matthew John Stephens.

How to Use *Exploring The World of Physics*

Students of several different ages and skill levels can use *Exploring the World of Physics*. Children in elementary grades can grasp many of the concepts, especially if given parental help.

Middle school students can enjoy the book independently and quickly test their understanding and comprehension by the challenge of answering the questions at the end of each chapter.

Junior high and high school students can revisit the book as a refresher course. The sections marked "For More Study" are intended to challenge older students. These sidebars can be a springboard for additional study by advanced students.

Thought-provoking questions and problems are found throughout the book. The activities reinforce the essential principles of physics.

Master Books®
A Division of New Leaf Publishing Group
www.masterbooks.net

Table of Contents

Motion

Physics is the science that explores how energy acts on matter. Everything in the universe that we can experience with our senses is made of matter and energy. The Bible recognized this fact in Genesis 1:1–3. After God created earth (matter), He said, "Let there be light [energy]."

Matter has weight and occupies space. Energy can put matter in motion or change it in some way. Physics is sometimes described as the study of matter in motion, but physics is far more than that because physics includes exploring not only motion, but also sound, heat, light, electricity, magnetism, and nuclear energy.

Physics goes far back in time. Aristotle, an ancient Greek scientist, lived more than 2,000 years ago. The Greeks made an effort to gain knowledge through observation and reasoning. However, they seldom did experiments, which are observations that can be repeated under

PROBLEMS

1. How do modern scientists test new ideas?

2. What discovery helped clocks keep better time?

3. How did Galileo slow the motion of falling balls?

Can You Propose Solutions?

controlled conditions. Without experiments, they could not repeat what they observed to test their conclusions.

For instance, suppose they saw a leaf fall from a tree and later saw an apple fall from the same tree. They might speculate as to why the apple appeared to fall more quickly than the leaf, but they would not think to pick up an apple and a leaf and drop them together.

In addition, measurement is essential to good science. Scientists must be able to measure quantities such as weight, distance, time, temperature, electric current, and light intensity. Ancient people had few accurate scientific instruments, so they could not easily measure what they observed. Ancient scientists could only state what they discovered as general conclusions rather than precise scientific principles.

For example, they might see a heavily loaded cart roll down a hill and conclude that it gained speed. From one moment to the next, it rolled faster and faster. However, they had no accurate clocks, so they could not time the cart and measure its actual speed.

The first person to make real progress in understanding physics was Galileo, a scientist who lived in Italy almost 500 years ago. Like the Greeks, he had a brilliant and inquiring mind. In addition to thinking and observing, he was willing to experiment. Experiments are a great way to collect scientific information and test new discoveries.

Galileo entered the University of Pisa in 1581 to study medicine. Europe at that time was coming out of a period known as the Middle Ages. The Middle Ages were sometimes called the Dark Ages in Europe because learning had been in a deep decline. Most people—including leaders of countries—could neither read nor write.

In these dark days, scholars held in high regard the confident writings of Aristotle and other Greeks who lived almost 2,000 years earlier. People of the 1500s turned to ancient books as final authority on scientific matters. They saw no reason to question Aristotle's books or test his statements.

During his first year at the university, Galileo discovered an important principle that ancient Greeks had completely overlooked.

Students at Pisa began their day by going to chapel. One morning Galileo knelt and said his prayers in the dark chapel. He arose to watch a lamplighter light the candles in a lamp which was hanging 30 feet from the high ceiling.

Lighting the candles caused the lamp to move in a slow back and forth motion. As its motion died down, it seemed to take as long to make a small swing as a large one. Galileo timed the chandelier swing with his pulse.

Galileo returned to his room to try other pendulums. Experiments showed that the time for a complete swing was the same whether the arc was a small one or a large one.

Galileo's discovery is known as the principle of the pendulum. A principle is a law of science. In this case, Galileo had found that two pendulums of the same length would swing at the same rate regardless of how wide or shallow

Aristotle taught his students to learn through observation and reasoning.

Aristotle

Aristotle (Greek Philosopher, 384 – 322 B.C.) was a great thinker of the ancient world. He attended school at Plato's Academy in Athens, Greece. It was one of the best schools in the world. Aristotle learned to observe carefully, pose insightful questions, and use reason to form conclusions. He did not, however, learn to do experiments to reveal new facts. Doing an experiment required work with the hands, but Greek thinkers thought manual labor was the work of servants.

Aristotle stayed in Athens for 20 years, first as a student and then as a teacher. He returned to his home country of Macedonia and served as the private tutor of the young man who would become Alexander the Great. Alexander the Great grew up to become the greatest military general of the ancient world.

Aristotle and Alexander the Great became good friends. Alexander the Great gave Aristotle money to start his own school in Athens. Aristotle called his school the Lyceum. Aristotle lectured as he walked about in the garden with his students. He encouraged his students to test their observations with common sense and clear thinking.

Aristotle wrote a book about the systems of laws that govern countries. He believed education was essential to the survival of a nation. Aristotle said, "All who have meditated on the art of governing mankind are convinced that the fate of empires depends on the education of youth."

About 50 of Aristotle's books were preserved. Errors in his books are minor considering the vast number of subjects he discussed. However, scholars in Europe during the Middle Ages believed his books contained no errors and all knowledge could be found in them. Medieval scholars made few important new discoveries in science. Aristotle would have been appalled if he had known that future people would use his books as the final word on scientific questions.

Aristotle tutoring Alexander the Great who was fourteen years old at the time.

their arcs. Only by making the string longer could he lengthen the time needed to make one back and forth swing.

Ancient Greeks had not mentioned this discovery in any of their books. The 17-year-old Galileo had made a discovery they had completely overlooked. Galileo realized that the ancient Greeks did not have all of the answers.

Galileo's discovery of the principle of the pendulum turned out to have a useful application. In Galileo's time, only length and weight could be measured with any accuracy. Merchants sold cloth, ribbon, and rope by length. They sold grain, potatoes, and coal by weight. They had developed accurate scales and rulers for measuring these quantities, but other tools of science, especially a way to accurately measure time, had not yet been invented.

Short intervals of time were especially difficult to measure. The best clocks of Galileo's day had only hour hands. They could not keep time accurately to the minute or second.

The regular back and forth motion of the pendulum would eventually regulate a clock so time could be measured to the second. However, attaching a pendulum to a clock would not occur until 30 years after Galileo died.

Galileo's experiments with pendulums set him thinking about other forms of motion. Almost everything taught about motion came from the books of Aristotle.

Aristotle claimed that heavy objects fall more rapidly than light ones. A ball ten times as heavy as a lighter one would fall ten times faster. A rumor sprang up that Galileo dropped different size iron balls from the tower of Pisa. It was the Leaning Tower of Pisa even then. Both heavy and light iron balls that Galileo dropped struck the ground at the same time.

He may not have done this experiment, but he did do other ones that convinced him that all objects would fall at the same speed.

Everyone knew that a feather would fall more slowly than a lump of lead. Galileo had to explain this everyday observation. He believed that air resistance caused differences

Falling Objects

Try this experiment testing the speed of falling objects.

Test whether light and heavy objects fall at same or different speeds. Place a dime and a quarter in the palm of your hand. Stand where the floor is hardwood, tile, or another solid surface that is not covered with carpet or a rug. Quickly lower and pull away your hand so the two coins start falling to the floor at the same instant. Listen for their impact.

A quarter is about 2½ times as heavy as a dime. If Aristotle were correct, it would strike the floor well before the dime. However, sounds of the coins show that they strike the floor at nearly the same instant.

Astronaut and Feather

Galileo would have been eager to witness David Scott's experiment.

In 1971, David Scott, one of the *Apollo 15* astronauts who landed on the moon, showed television viewers back on earth an unusual experiment. Scott told them, "Galileo, a long time ago, made an important discovery about falling objects in gravity fields."

He held a falcon feather in his left hand. In his right hand, he held a hammer. Scott let go of the hammer and feather at the same moment.

On earth, the feather would have floated down because of air resistance. On the moon with no atmosphere to slow the feather, it fell at the same speed as the hammer. They fell side by side and hit the surface of the moon at the same time.

in speed. To test his idea, he beat a ball of lead into a thin sheet. When he dropped the sheet, it fluttered down more slowly than a lead ball of the same weight.

Galileo suggested that in a vacuum where air was not present, the feather and lump of lead would fall side by side. Critics of Galileo thought his idea could never be tested. Aristotle had said a vacuum was impossible: "Nature abhors [dislikes] a vacuum." However, about 50 years later, an English scientist named Robert Boyle built an air pump. He put a lump of lead and a feather inside a glass tube. He pumped out the air and turned the tube over. The feather and lead fell at the same speed.

Galileo continued to experiment with how quickly objects fell to earth. To do this he needed to measure speed. Speed is distance per time interval—meters per second, feet per second, or miles per hour. Meters, feet, and miles are measures of distance. Seconds and hours are measures of time.

The speed of an object is found by dividing the distance it travels by the time it takes to go that distance: speed = distance/time. The slash mark, /, is read "divided by."

To calculate speed, divide distance by time. For instance, an automobile that travels 200 miles in four hours, travels at an average speed of 50 miles per hour: speed = distance/time = 200 miles/4 hours = 50 mi/hr. In the expression 50 mi/hr, the slash mark is read as "per." The car could have a speed of 35 mi/hr during part of the trip, and 65 mi/hr during some other part of the trip. The speed of 50 mi/hr is the average speed for the entire four hours.

Speed is always measured as distance divided by time. A high school runner would be pleased with finishing the 100-meter dash in 10.6 seconds. The runner's speed is 100 meters divided by 10.6 seconds or 9.35 m/sec.

The "miles per hour" or "meters per second" are units of speed. Scientists know that units are an important part of the overall quantity and always state them. Without units, the number part is meaningless. To say that a car was doing 90 could be fast (90 miles per hour) or slower

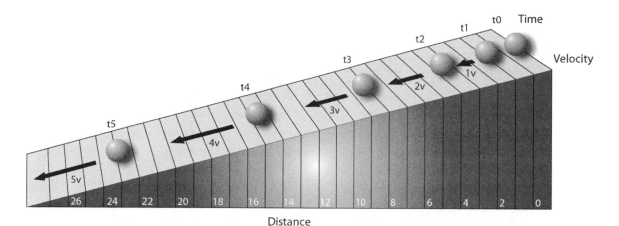

Galileo rolled steel balls down a gently sloping incline. He measured the distances moved in equal intervals of time using a water clock. Velocity increased uniformly with time as the ball moved down the incline under the force of gravity.

(90 feet per second, about 61 miles per hour). In a European country, it could be 90 kilometers per hour, which is about 56 miles per hour.

Galileo became interested in measuring how quickly objects fell to earth. For an object to fall for five seconds, he would need a tower 400 feet high. The Leaning Tower of Pisa was only 180 feet high. Even with a high tower, objects would fall too rapidly for him to measure their speed accurately.

Galileo found an inventive solution. Rather than dropping a ball, he rolled one down a ramp. A ramp with a gentle slope would lessen the force of gravity. When dropped from a height, a ball fell 16 feet in the first second, but on a gently sloping ramp that is 16 feet long and two feet high, a ball took eight seconds to roll 16 feet. Its motion could be studied in detail at slower speed.

Measuring time was still a problem because Galileo had no accurate clock. He again found a creative solution. While the ball rolled down the ramp, he allowed water to escape from a hole in the bottom of a container. Then he weighed the water—accurate scales did exist. He measured time by weight of the water.

The last problem was to limit friction. Galileo made smooth bronze balls and highly polished wooden tracks. Friction became so minor as to be ignored.

After Galileo collected his data, he set about seeing what he could learn. He ana-

lyzed the data, and he noticed that the ball rolling down the ramp did not get up to speed instantly. Instead, it started slowly and continued to gain speed all the way down the ramp. Falling objects followed the same rule. They began falling slowly and then continued to gain speed as they fell.

After he understood the effect of gravity on balls rolling down a ramp, he calculated distance, speed, and acceleration of a freely falling body for each second of travel. (See Table: Motion of Falling Objects.)

In the first column, Galileo recorded total time in seconds. The second column shows the distance the ball fell at the end of each second. Next, Galileo calculated average speed by dividing distance by time. For instance, in the last row, time is five seconds and distance is 400 feet, so the average speed is 80 feet per second: speed = distance / time = 400 ft/5 sec = 80 ft/sec.

The third column has the final speed at the end of each second. The final speed is greater than the average speed because the falling ball is constantly gaining speed.

The average of two numbers is found by dividing their sum by two. If the first number is zero, then the average is merely one-half of the second number. In Galileo's experiment, the balls started at rest, so their beginning speed was zero. Their average speed was one half of the final speed, which is another way of saying final speed was twice as great as

Table: Motion of Falling Objects				
Time seconds	Distance feet	Average speed ft/sec	Final Speed ft/sec	Acceleration of Gravity ft/sec^2
1	16	16	32	32
2	64	32	64	32
3	144	48	96	32
4	256	64	128	32
5	400	80	160	32

average speed. For five seconds, the falling object has an average speed of 80 ft/sec. The final speed was twice 80 ft/sec, or 160 ft/sec.

Notice final speeds at the end of each second: 32 ft/sec, 64 ft/sec, 96 ft/sec, 138 ft/sec, and 160 ft/sec. Galileo discovered something very interesting. Each speed differed from the previous one by 32: 64 – 32 = 32; 96 – 64 = 32, 128 – 96 = 32, and 160 – 128 = 32.

The last column shows acceleration due to gravity, which is one of Galileo's important discoveries. Acceleration due to gravity on earth is written as 32 ft/sec^2. This quantity can be read as 32 feet per second per second or 32 feet per second squared. In the metric system, the acceleration due to gravity is 9.81 m/sec^2.

Acceleration is the change in speed compared to the time taken for the speed to change. Acceleration is found by dividing the change in speed by the change in time: acceleration = (change in speed)/(change in time). Acceleration compares how speed changes with time, and speed compares how distance changes with time.

People find acceleration confusing, and with good reason. Acceleration is the rate at which another rate (speed) changes, but acceleration is not speed, nor is it even a change in speed. Instead, it is the change in speed compared to the change in time. Time is squared because it appears twice in the calculation of acceleration.

Units of time for acceleration are usually the same, such as sec^2, but different units of time can be used. For instance, a high-speed drag racer goes from zero miles per hour to 300 miles per hour in about five seconds. The dragster increases its speed by about 60 miles per hour every second. Acceleration = (change in speed)/(change in time) = (300 mi/hr)/(5 sec) = 60 mi/hr per sec, or 60 mi/hr × sec. After the first second, the dragster is going 60 miles per hour.

Units of time for acceleration of the dragster are not the same. One is in hours and the other is in seconds. The units for this acceleration are mi/hr × sec because both the hours and seconds are in the denominators of the fractions. They are multiplied together.

Galileo's discoveries about motions of objects on earth had a strong impact on scientists of his day. He replaced centuries of argument and speculation with a few simple equations that led to a much better understanding of motion.

Galileo studied the motion of cannonballs blasted from a cannon. Projectile motion had been poorly understood until he proved that a cannonball followed a curving path known as a parabola. It was part of a series of geometric curves known as conic sections that had been studied in detail for centuries. Because the parabola was so well understood, the paths of projectiles became easy to calculate.

Galileo's discovery about cannonballs applied to any object that was fired or thrown.

For More Study — Final and Average Velocity

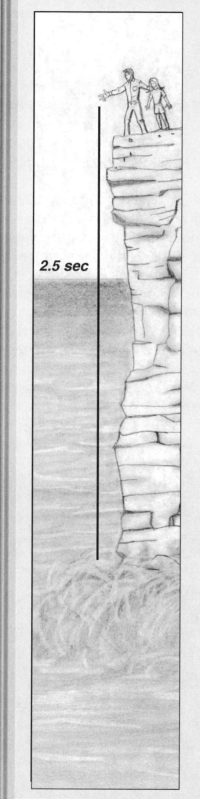

2.5 sec

Suppose you toss a pebble from a cliff into the ocean and notice that the pebble falls for 2.5 seconds before it strikes the surface of the water. How high is the cliff?

One way to solve this problem is to first calculate the final velocity using the equation $v_f = g \times t$, where vf is the final velocity, g is the acceleration of gravity, and t is the time.

$$v_f = g \times t$$
$$v_f = (32 \text{ ft/sec}^2) \times (2.5 \text{ sec})$$
$$v_f = 80 \text{ ft/sec}$$

Next, calculate the average speed from the equation $v_{ave} = \frac{1}{2} \times v_f$, with v_{ave} standing for average velocity:

$$v_{ave} = \frac{1}{2} v_f$$
$$v_{ave} = \frac{1}{2} \, 80 \text{ ft/sec}$$
$$v_{ave} = 40 \text{ ft/sec}$$

Finally, calculate the total distance with the equation $d = v_{ave} \times t$, with d the distance, v_{ave} the average velocity, and t the time.

$$d = v_{ave} \times t$$
$$d = 40 \text{ ft/sec} \times 2.5 \text{ sec}$$
$$d = 100 \text{ ft}$$

The answer of 100 feet is correct, although it took three steps to find the answer. Distance an object falls in 2.5 seconds can be found by a single equation. The three equations shown above can be combined into a single equation to give distance:

$$d = v_{ave} \times t$$
$$d = (\tfrac{1}{2} v_f) \times t \qquad \text{replace } v_{ave} \text{ with } \tfrac{1}{2}v_f$$
$$d = \tfrac{1}{2} (g \times t) \times t \qquad \text{replace } v_f \text{ with } g \times t$$
$$d = \tfrac{1}{2} g \times t^2 \qquad \text{replace } g \text{ with } 32 \text{ ft/sec}^2$$

The equation $d = \frac{1}{2} g \times t^2$ can now be used to find distance:

$$d = \tfrac{1}{2} (32 \text{ ft/sec}^2) \times (2.5 \text{ sec})^2$$
$$d = 16 \text{ ft/sec} \times 6.25 \text{ sec}^2$$
$$d = 100 \text{ ft}$$

By the way, many processes in physics are reversible. Instead of dropping a pebble, suppose you threw it straight up in the air. If it takes 2.5 seconds before its upward motion stops, then it left your hand at 80 ft/sec, and it will go 100 feet into the air.

Galileo established that a projectile would travel its greatest distance if fired at an angle of 45 degrees — halfway from the horizontal to directly overhead. Today, athletes practice throwing the shot put, discus, and javelin at this angle for the greatest range. You can experiment with a stream of water squirted from a garden hose to see that this rule is true.

Galileo and his telescope

Scientists are pleased when they find a way to replace what appear to be many different observations with a single, simple principle. Galileo's simple and concise equations applied to many different types of motion. Nature, rather than being a head-scratching puzzlement, proved to follow a few simple principles. Galileo showed that nature had been given a design that human beings could understand.

Galileo is best known for his discoveries with a telescope, although his experiments measuring the speed of balls rolling down ramps are just as important. He did not invent the telescope, but he was the first to use it to study the heavens. He made a small telescope and turned it to the night sky. He saw mountains and valleys on the moon, four large satellites orbiting the planet Jupiter, and many stars too dim to see with eyes alone.

Scientists and teachers refused to look through his telescope. They argued, "Aristotle tells nothing of them. They must be the fault of Galileo's glass." Galileo said, "I have offered a thousand times to show the leading philosophers my studies. They will not consent to look at the planets or moon through the telescope. They close their eyes to the light of truth!"

Jealous professors tried to discredit him. They implied that he was trying to prove that the Bible was wrong.

Their charge was groundless. His argument was with those scientists who blindly followed Aristotle. Galileo charged that Aristotle had made mistakes, not prophets of God.

Galileo spent the last part of his life under house arrest. He used his time to meet with friends and to train students. Galileo wrote a book about his discoveries called *The Starry Messenger*. Professors banded together and forced Galileo to stop publishing his books for many years.

Galileo planted seeds of doubt about Aristotle and other Greek philosophers whose ideas had brought scientific progress to a halt. Galileo's stubborn insistence upon experiments and careful observations blossomed into a new spirit of discovery known as the Scientific Revolution.

Galileo was deeply religious. He believed that none of his theories dishonored any of the facts in the Bible. His faith in God grew stronger, not weaker, because his telescope showed such a marvelous universe.

SOLUTIONS

1. They do experiments to test new ideas.

2. The principle of the pendulum measures seconds.

3. Ramps slowed the motion.

Galileo's equations described many different types of motion.

Questions

A B C D   1.   Physics is the science that explores how energy acts on (A. heat   B. light C. matter   D. sound).

T F   2.   The ancient Greeks were noted for their careful experiments.

T F   3.   The regular back and forth motion of a pendulum was used to regulate the first accurate clocks.

T F   4.   In Galileo's time, only length and time could be measured with any accuracy.

A B C D   5.   A feather and lump of lead will fall at the same speed in (A. a high speed wind tunnel   B. the atmosphere   C. a vacuum   D. water).

6.   To calculate speed, divide distance by _____.

A B C D   7.   To study the motion of falling objects, Galileo (A. beat them into cubes B. dropped them from a high tower   C. pushed them from a cliff D. rolled them down a ramp).

A B C D   8.   Acceleration is found by dividing the (A. average velocity   B. distance C. gravity   D. change in speed) by the change in time.

A B   9.   On earth, the acceleration due to gravity is (A. 32 ft/sec^2 B. 60 miles/hour).

For More Study

10.   Suppose a canoeist takes 70 days to paddle the entire length of the Mississippi River, a distance of 3,710 miles. The canoeist's average speed in miles per day is _____.

11.   An ordinary passenger car can accelerate to 60 miles per hour in about eight seconds. What is the car's acceleration?

12.   On the moon, the acceleration due to gravity is 5.3 ft/sec^2 rather than 32 ft/sec^2. If an object fell six seconds before hitting the ground, it strikes the ground with a speed of _____ ft/sec. (Hint: use the final velocity equation.)

Chapter Two

Laws of Motion

Despite Galileo's success, much still needed to be understood about motion. Scientists began using a variety of terms that were poorly understood and seldom scientifically defined: velocity, acceleration, force, weight, mass, and inertia.

For instance, speed and velocity do not mean the same-thing. Velocity of an object includes not only its speed but also its direction. For a car to have constant velocity, it must travel at a constant speed in an unchanging direction. A car going 60 miles per hour along a straight and level highway has constant speed and velocity. A car traveling at the same speed around a curve does not have constant velocity because its direction changes.

As another example, the moon travels in an orbit around earth at a nearly constant speed, but its velocity is continually changing because the moon's straight-line course is bent as it orbits earth.

PROBLEMS

1. How does a push or pull change motion?

2. Why do dump trucks have powerful engines?

3. Why does a ball player follow through as he swings a bat?

Can You Propose Solutions?

Force is another word that has a specific meaning in physics. We all have an idea of the meaning of the term "force." Force of gravity pulls on us. Force of friction slows moving objects. Force of a magnet attracts metal paperclips.

Force is a push or pull that changes an object's velocity. Force is needed to put an object in motion, give it greater speed, or slow it down. Force is also needed to change its direction. In every case, the velocity of the object changes. A force must act on an object to change its velocity.

Galileo died in 1642 in Italy. That same year, Isaac Newton, a brilliant scientist, was born in England. Isaac Newton used information collected by Galileo to develop three laws of motion. In expressing these laws, he also clearly explained what he meant by force, mass, inertia, and several other terms.

In one experiment, Galileo rolled a ball down a ramp, across a level track, and then back up a ramp on the other side. He saw that the ball gained speed going down the track, ran at constant speed going across the table on a level track, and lost speed when it ran back up a ramp on the other side.

Until then, people believed that a moving object would naturally slow. Some force had to keep it going.

Galileo concluded the opposite. A moving object keeps going in a straight line at the same speed. Rather than a force being needed to keep it going, a force would be needed to slow it, speed it, or change its direction.

True, a ball rolling on a flat surface does slow. Friction is the force that slows it. Galileo believed that a ball rolling across a perfectly level and frictionless table would keep moving without gaining or losing speed. It would slow, speed up, or change direction only when a force acted on it.

Isaac Newton recognized the importance of Galileo's discovery and stated it as his first law of motion.

First Law of Motion: An object at rest will remain at rest and an object in motion

Portrait of Isaac Newton

will remain in straight-line motion at constant speed unless acted upon by an unbalanced force.

What is an unbalanced force? It is the force remaining after all other forces have been taken into account. For an object to move as described in law one, it is not necessary for no forces to act upon it, but for the combination of forces to equal zero. Sometimes "unbalanced" force is called an "outside" force.

For example, an airplane in flight experiences four forces: forward thrust of propeller, backward force of air friction (called drag), upward lift of wings, and downward pull of gravity, called weight. If thrust equals drag and lift equals weight, then the airplane has no unbalanced forces. It flies straight and level at a uniform speed.

People in Newton's day saw events that appeared to prove wrong the first law. Heavy carts rolled to a stop unless strong draft horses continued to pull them. Apples fell from a tree with no visible force acting on them. Sailing ships tended to drift off course. In each case a force was in action. Force of friction slowed the cart; force of gravity caused objects to drop to the ground; and force of wind or ocean currents carried ships off course. Force of friction, wind, and gravity all caused objects to gain or lose speed or change direction.

Most people become aware of the first law of motion only when they are on a surface that is nearly free of friction. A driver who must travel on an icy pavement for the first time has trouble putting the car in motion, slowing it down, or making a turn. The car wants to keep its straight-line motion according to the first law.

The first law of motion is sometimes called the law of inertia. Inertia is the tendency of an object to resist acceleration; that is, changes in its velocity. It is the property of matter that causes an object to remain at rest, or if in motion to stay in motion in a straight line unless acted on by an outside force.

The First Law of Motion: A vehicle is streamlined to reduce the force of air resistance so the vehicle will more fully take advantage of the first law of motion.

Every object has inertia. How much depends upon the amount of matter an object contains. More matter means more inertia. A skateboard has a small amount of inertia compared to an automobile. A skateboard rolls with a slight push, but an automobile needs more effort to get it moving.

The first law of motion can be written in mathematical shorthand as: $f = 0$ then $a = 0$, with f standing for force and a standing for acceleration. If force acts directly along an object's line of motion, then the object will gain speed. If force acts opposite the motion (as the force of friction always does), then the object will slow. When you slide a book across a table and it comes to a stop, the force of friction slows the book. Reducing speed is also acceleration, although it is sometimes called negative acceleration or deceleration.

A force that acts directly from the side will not change the speed of an object, but will change its direction. This, too, is acceleration because acceleration is any change in speed or direction. If

The Four Forces Acting on an Airplane in Flight

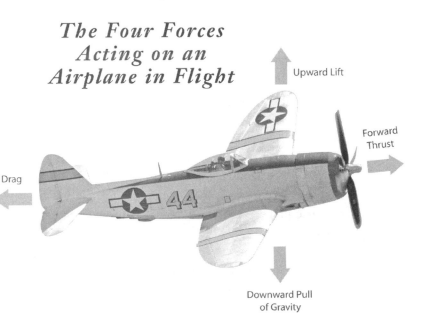

Upward Lift

Forward Thrust

Drag

Downward Pull of Gravity

An airplane in flight experiences four forces: forward thrust of propeller, drag, upward lift of wings, and downward pull of gravity.

you take a ball attached to a string and whirl it around over your head at a constant speed, the ball is being accelerated. The tension of the string is a force that pulls the ball out of its straight-line path.

In addition to force, Newton also realized that mass affects acceleration. He noticed that a small buggy could be pulled by a single horse, but a heavily loaded wagon required a team of horses. More mass required more force to get it moving. He stated his observations about acceleration, force, and mass as the second law of motion.

Second Law of Motion: The acceleration of an object is directly proportional to the force acting on it and inversely proportional to its mass.

In symbols, the second law can be stated as: $a = f/m$, with a the acceleration, f the force, and m the mass. The equation shows that acceleration and force are directly related to one another. Doubling force doubles acceleration, provided mass stays the same.

In the equation $a = f/m$, acceleration is in the numerator and mass is in the denominator. Mass and acceleration are inversely proportional. As one increases, the other decreases. An increase in mass reduces acceleration, provided the force does not change. A fully loaded dump truck is harder to accelerate than the same empty truck. It has more mass but the same engine.

On the other hand, if mass is reduced, the same force causes greater acceleration. Reducing mass in vehicles improves performance. They accelerate more quickly, turn more easily, and go farther on the same amount of gas. Mass can be reduced by replacing heavier steel with lighter aluminum or other alloys. Lighter cars equipped with the same engine have better acceleration. Their improved performance is a direct result of Newton's second law of motion.

Mass and weight are not the same. Mass is a measure of inertia. Weight is a measure of the force of gravitational attraction. To show that they are different, the metric system uses kilograms to measure mass, but a unit called

Demonstrate Inertia

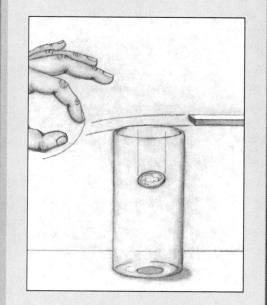

Try this experiment showing the effects of inertia.

Place a piece of stiff cardboard over a glass and rest a coin on the card. Thump the card quickly. What do you observe? The card flies away and the coin drops into the glass. Friction between the card and coin is too slight to overcome the coin's inertia. Inertia of the coin keeps it in place until the card is removed, then the force of gravity causes the coin to fall into the cup.

the newton (named after Isaac Newton, of course) to measure weight. In the English system, most people use the pound to measure both mass and weight.

Mass and weight are independent of one another. A student who weighs 90 pounds on earth weighs 15 pounds on the moon and zero pounds floating in space. Yet, his mass is the same in all three locations.

Often, the second law of motion, $a = f/m$, is rewritten as the force equation: $f = m \times a$. Isaac Newton replaced the vague idea of force as a push or pull with a specific way to calculate its value. To measure the strength of a force acting on an object, measure the mass of the object and the amount of acceleration. Force is the product of mass and acceleration. In the metric system, one newton of force gives one kilogram of mass an acceleration of one meter per second squared: $1.0 \text{ n} = 1.0 \text{ kg} \times \text{m/sec}^2$.

In the second law, Isaac Newton showed that force is necessary to cause an object to change speed or direction. In his third law of motion, Newton states that such forces always come in pairs. The two forces are equal but opposite in direction.

Third Law of Motion: To every action there is an equal and opposite reaction.

Young children often learn the truth of the third law of motion when they try to jump from a small wagon. If they jump out the back, the wagon suddenly flies forward, and they take a tumble to the ground.

Even adults may forget the third law of motion. Suppose a person jumps from a boat to the dock before the boat is safely tied to the landing. The person goes one way, the boat goes the other, and the person often lands in the water.

Perhaps Newton himself observed such an event. The Cam River flowed through Cambridge, the town where he attended college. Or perhaps in winter he watched ice skaters. Because of the greatly reduced friction, the three laws of motion are easily experienced on ice.

Suppose two people are standing still at the center of a frozen pond. They push against one another. Each skater experiences a force. The two forces are equal in size but opposite in direction. The skaters separate in opposite directions. If they are the same size and have the same mass, they separate at the same speed. But if one is larger than the other, the person with the smaller mass will accelerate away at a higher speed.

Regardless of how he came up with the third law, Isaac Newton offered a simple

The Second Law of Motion: A massive vehicle needs a powerful engine to make it accelerate.

The Third Law of Motion: A rocket moves forward because hot gases are expelled at great speed in the opposite direction.

example. He said, "If you press a stone with your finger, the finger is also pressed by the stone."

Another example of the third law of motion is the action of a balloon when the air inside it is released. The balloon flies about until all of the air is exhausted. The gases escaping in one direction cause the balloon to zoom in the other direction.

The third law of motion can be stated as an equation: $f_{ab} = -f_{ba}$, and is read as the force of object a on object b is equal but opposite to the force of object b on object a.

Two concepts closely related to the third law are impulse and momentum. Impulse is the product of force and the length of time force is applied. The equation for impulse is $I = f \times t$, with I the impulse, f the force and t the time.

Coaches encourage their players to "follow through." Whether the player swings a tennis racket, golf club, or bat, the idea is to keep the swing going after the ball makes contact. The reason is simple: The longer a force is applied, the greater the change in velocity. A baseball player who keeps the force of his bat in contact

Impulse and momentum, which are closely related to the third law of motion, are utilized by ball players when they follow through with their bat after hitting the ball.

Rockets and the Third Law of Motion

During the early 1900s, Robert Goddard of the United States experimented with rocket flight. Starting in 1909, he built rocket motors in his laboratory and tested them. He drew pictures in his notebooks of rockets looping around the moon. Most people dismissed the idea as wildly impractical. Some called him moon mad.

Robert continued his experiments for 20 years. He built the first rocket engine to burn liquid fuel. One of his rockets carried the first scientific payload. It carried instruments to measure temperature and atmospheric pressure, and a camera to take photographs while in flight. In 1927, he built larger rockets at a test site in New Mexico. For 10 years, Robert carried out experiments that led to success after success, although none reached into space.

The New York Times newspaper claimed that a rocket motor wouldn't operate in the emptiness of space. The newspaper said, "The motor would have nothing to push against." About Goddard, the newspaper said, "He doesn't know the relation of action to reaction. He lacks the knowledge ladled out daily in high school."

Robert Goddard fully understood Newton's third law of motion. Years earlier, he had settled the question of whether a rocket could operate in the vacuum of space. While still in college, he pumped air out of a long pipe. He fired a small rocket motor inside. As hot gases escaped from the engine, they pushed the rocket forward. The engine developed thrust in a vacuum.

The third law does not require the hot gases to push against anything. In fact, a rocket motor actually works better in space. Without the conflicting force of air pressure, hot gases spew out of the engine even faster. The rocket accelerates better in the vacuum of space than it does in earth's atmosphere.

with the ball for twice as long will give the ball an impulse twice as great.

Watch a cat land on its feet and you will see that it bends its knees to absorb energy. Its contact with the floor is spread over a greater period of time. This reduces the force of the impact. Skydivers learn to bend their knees as they land. By spreading force over a greater period of time, there is less chance of an injury.

Final velocity of a rocket depends upon force produced by the rocket engine and length of time force is given. The main engines of the space shuttle provided a huge 1.2 million pounds of thrust, but they burn fuel for only eight minutes. Engineers have designed other engines for use in spacecraft that travel between planets. The engines generate only a few ounces of thrust, but do so for days on end.

Isaac Newton also defined the concept of momentum. Momentum is the mass of an object times its velocity: momentum = $m \times v$. Usually, the letter p is used for momentum because the letter m is used for mass, so the equation can be written as $p = m \times v$, with p the momentum, m the mass, and v the velocity.

When two football players collide, the larger player has the advantage because of his greater mass. The larger player has more mass and greater momentum provided the two players are running at the same speed. On the other hand, if an offensive player hits the line fast enough, his extra speed may give him enough momentum to break through the line even if he is not as heavy as the defenders.

The third law of motion states that for every action there is an equal and forcible reaction. The third law can be stated in terms of momentum. In fact, Isaac Newton originally stated the third law of motion in terms of the gain and loss of momentum. He said that if one object gains momentum, then the other object must lose an equal amount of momentum and in the opposite direction.

As an example, when a batter swings at a ball, the ball is going in one direction at a certain speed. After the bat hits the ball, the ball is going in a different direction at a different speed. Because its velocity has changed, so has the ball's momentum. The momentum of the bat changes by the same amount, but in the opposite direction.

Scientists have discovered that no matter how objects collide, total momentum before a collision is equal to total momentum after a collision. This is known as the law of conservation of momentum. It is one of the most firmly established laws of science.

Normally, we think of the word conservation as meaning to be frugal, to save, to protect natural resources, or otherwise make the best use of something. In physics, however, conservation has a very specific meaning. It means that in a closed system, certain measurable quantities are constant. A closed system is an area protected from outside forces.

Imagine two large, perfectly round jellybeans rolling toward one another. Each one weighs one kilogram (about 2.2 pounds). One is rolling to the east at five meters per second. The other is rolling to the west at the same speed. The two jellybeans hit one another head on and stick together. Because each one has

For More Study— Momentum

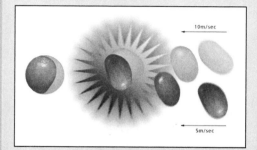

Colliding jellybeans show the effects of inertia

Suppose two jellybeans of equal mass (1 kg) are going in the same direction but at different speeds. One is going to the east (positive) at 10 m/sec and it overtakes another jellybean also going to the east (positive) at 5 m/sec. They collide and stick together to form a larger, perfectly round jellybean. What will be its speed?

First calculate the momentum before the collision. Let p_b represent the total momentum before collision and p_1 and p_2 the momentum of the first and second jellybean.

$$p_b = p_1 + p_2$$
$$p_b = m_1 \times v_1 + m_2 \times v_2$$
$$p_b = 1 \text{ kg} \times 10 \text{ m/sec} + 1 \text{ kg} \times 5 \text{ m/sec}$$
$$p_b = 15 \text{ kg m/sec}$$

After the collision there is a single jellybean that has a mass, m_a, of 2 kg. The momentum after the collision, p_a, is the same as before the collision, 15 kg m/sec. The velocity after, v_a, can be calculated given the momentum and mass.

$$p_a = m_a \times v_a$$
$$15 \text{ kg} \times \text{m/sec} = 2 \text{ kg} \times v_a$$
$$7.5 \text{ m/sec} = v_a$$

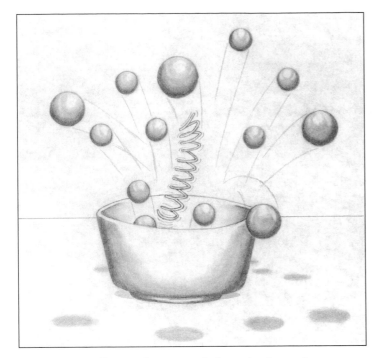

Collision does not violate the law of conservation of momentum.

the same momentum, each cancels the other's momentum and they come to a dead stop.

Does this collision violate the law of conservation of momentum? No, because momentum is a vector quantity. In physics, a vector is any quantity that has size and direction. Momentum is a vector because it has two parts: mass and velocity. To completely give the velocity of an object, both the speed and direction must be stated. In the expression "5 m/sec east," 5 m/sec is the speed and east is the direction.

Going back to the jellybeans, one rolled east and the other rolled west. They had equal weights and equal speeds, but their momentums had opposite signs because they traveled in opposite directions. Overall, the total momentum before the collision was zero, the same as after the collision.

As another example, imagine a spring coiled up in a bowl of marbles. The spring suddenly uncoils, sending the marbles flying every which way. Suppose you could measure the mass, speed, and direction of each marble. What would be the total momentum of all the marbles? You don't need to do the calculation, because before the marbles were tossed about by the spring, the bowl of marbles had zero momentum. After the spring was released,

they would still have zero total momentum. Momentum is conserved.

One of the key concepts of physics is the idea of conservation. Some quantities such as momentum cannot be changed. The universe began with a certain supply of momentum and we cannot add to it nor subtract from it. No matter how objects collide, total momentum remains the same. If one object gains momentum, then another object must lose momentum.

Chemists found that a similar law applied to matter. During a chemical reaction, total weight of ingredients equaled total weight of products. Chemists stated the law of conservation of matter. During ordinary chemical reactions, matter can neither be created nor destroyed but merely changed into different compounds.

Momentum, energy, matter, and electric charge are conserved. Other quantities on the subatomic level of elementary particles are also conserved. The fact that conservation laws exist is because of the underlying design in nature.

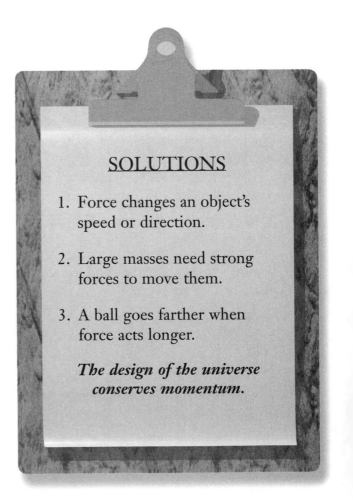

SOLUTIONS

1. Force changes an object's speed or direction.

2. Large masses need strong forces to move them.

3. A ball goes farther when force acts longer.

The design of the universe conserves momentum.

T F	1.	Velocity and speed mean the same.
T F	2.	A force must act on an object to put the object in motion, give it greater speed, slow it, or change its direction.
T F	3.	All objects come to a stop unless some force keeps them going.
A B	4.	A ball rolling on a flat surface comes to a stop because of the force of (A. friction B. gravity).
A B C	5.	Isaac Newton's first law of motion was based on experiments done by (A. Aristotle B. Galileo C. Newton himself).
A B C D	6.	Inertia is a property of matter that resists changing its (A. electric charge B. mass C. momentum D. velocity).
T F	7.	Only very massive objects have inertia.
T F	8.	Acceleration is any change of speed or direction.
	9.	State the second law of motion:
	10.	State the third law of motion:
	11.	Momentum is the mass of an object times its _____.
T F	12.	The law of conservation of momentum is one of the most firmly established laws of science.

Matching

13. _____ first law of motion
14. _____ second law of motion
15. _____ third law of motion
16. _____ force equation
17. _____ definition of impulse
18. _____ definition of momentum

a. $a = f/m$
b. $f = m \times a$
c. $f_{ab} = -f_{ba}$
d. $I = f \times t$
e. If $f = 0$ then $a = 0$
f. $p = m \times v$

Gravity

Astronomy is a branch of physics that explores the universe, and the sun, moon, stars, gas, and dust that composes it.

At about the same time that Galileo explored motions of objects on earth, Johannes Kepler made equally important calculations about motions of planets. Galileo had to constantly deal with the problem of friction, but objects in space move freely without friction. In fact, their motions differed so greatly from those on earth that most people believed two different sets of laws were at work — one for earthly objects and another for heavenly objects.

Kepler and many other scientists such as Galileo and Isaac Newton believed in a design in nature — a design put there by the Creator. They strived to replace confusing and contradictory scientific information with simple and easy-to-understand principles.

PROBLEMS

1. Why did Kepler fail at first to calculate the orbit of Mars?

2. How are motions in space and those on earth alike?

3. How can astronomers find unseen planets around distant stars?

Can You Propose Solutions?

The First Law of Planetary Motion: Each planet orbits the sun in an elliptical path. Here the elliptical paths of the earth, three planets and Halley's comet are shown.

Johannes Kepler studied the Bible at a University in Germany and planned upon being a minister of the gospel. While a student, Johannes Kepler took a class in astronomy.

Johannes Kepler learned how to calculate when the moon would be full, when the sun would rise and set, when eclipses would darken the sun. He knew that God had given the sun, moon, stars, and planets as natural clocks and calendars. The Bible in Genesis 1:14 says, "…let them be for signs, and for seasons, and for days, and years."

Kepler possessed exceptional skill as a mathematician. A school in Graz, Austria, asked him to work there as a mathematics teacher. At the urging of Christian friends, he accepted the job. As part of his duties, he wrote a yearly calendar and almanac. An almanac helped farmers and travelers by predicting time of sunrise, sunset, full moon, and events about the planets.

Kepler believed in a basic harmony of the universe put there by the Creator. He believed that God had created the laws that governed nature. As His special creation, human beings should be able to trace out those laws and understand nature. Yet, the motion of the planets proved to be exceptionally difficult to understand.

From the time of the ancient Greeks, astronomers believed planets traveled in perfectly circular orbits at constant speeds. However, a single circle could not account for all of the motions of a particular planet, such as Mars, so more circles were added to the scheme.

Despite his best efforts, Kepler's calculations fell short of predicting the path of Mars correctly. After years of effort, Kepler realized his stubborn error. He along with all other astronomers believed Mars traveled in a circle around the sun. What if Mars' orbit was a figure other than a perfect circle?

Johannes Kepler proved that Mars traveled around the sun in a stretched-out figure called an ellipse.

In 1609, Johannes Kepler told about his discoveries in his book, *The New Astronomy*. The book contained two of his three laws of planetary motion. He ended the book with a song of praise for the Creator. He wrote, "Thus God himself was too kind to remain idle, and began to play the game of signatures, signing His likeness into the world."

Johannes Kepler enjoyed great fame during his lifetime. His fame continues to grow. On any list of great scientists, he is usually in the top ten. He considered his vast scientific studies as another way of looking into God's magnificent creation. He often became so excited with his discoveries that he would write songs of praise to God in his scientific journals.

Kepler's three laws of planetary motion became the foundation of modern astronomy.

First Law of Planetary Motion: Each planet orbits the sun in an elliptical path. The sun is at one focus of the ellipse.

The first law gave the shape of a planet's orbit as an ellipse. An ellipse has two points along the main axis called foci. Kepler showed that the sun was at one of the foci. The other focus was empty.

Kepler carefully plotted the orbit of Mars using 20 observations of the planet taken the same number of days apart. He connected pairs of points on the ellipse with the point of the sun. The lines made triangles that differed in shape because the planet did not travel at equal speeds everywhere in its orbit. It traveled faster when it was closer to the sun. On the other side of the ellipse, when farther from the sun, it traveled slower.

The lines made triangles that differed in shape. Suppose you ran a line from the sun to the planet when it was on the side of the ellipse nearest the sun. In a certain period of time, say ten days, its greater speed would cause the line to sweep out a broad but thick triangle. Then on the other side of the ellipse, the planet would travel slower. Once again, connect a line from the planet to the sun. This time it would sweep out in ten days a thin and long triangle. Yet, Kepler calculated that each triangle — one short and fat, the other long and thin — had the same area. This gave his second law of planetary motion.

Second Law of Planetary Motion: The straight line joining a planet with the sun sweeps out equal areas in equal intervals of time.

In 1619, Kepler published his book *Harmony of the Worlds*, in which he showed that Jupiter's moons traveled in elliptical orbits, but with Jupiter taking the place of the sun. The earth's own moon also traveled around the earth in an elliptical orbit. In the book, Kepler also stated the third of law of planetary motion.

Third Law of Planetary Motion: The cube of a planet's distance from the sun divided by the square of its period of revolution is a constant and is the same for all planets.

As an equation, Kepler's third law can be written as $d^3/t^2 = k$ with d the average distance from the sun, t the time it takes for the planet to go around the sun (its period of revolution), and k a constant that is the same for all planets. The equation shows that the farther a planet is from the sun, the slower it travels, and the longer it takes to make a complete orbit.

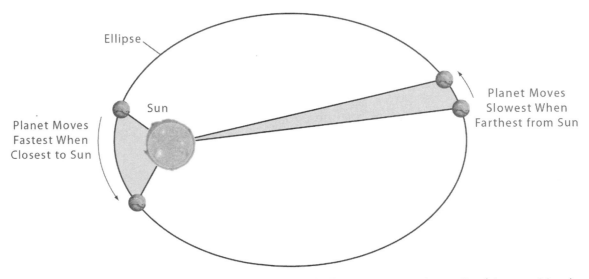

The Second Law of Planetary Motion: The straight line joining a planet (in this case Mars) with the sun sweeps out equal areas in equal intervals of time.

Planets	Time to Orbit the Sun	Astronomical Units (using Kepler's equation of the earth's distance =1.0)	
Mercury	87.97 days	0.39	about $4/10$ as far from the sun as the earth
Venus	227.54 days	0.72	about $3/4$ as far from the sun as the earth
Earth	265.25 days	1.00	the earth's distance is set equal to 1.0
Mars	686.98 days	1.52	about $1\ 1/2$ times as far from the sun as the earth
Jupiter	11.86 years	5.20	a little more than 5 times as far from the sun as the earth
Saturn	29.46 years	9.52	almost 10 times as far from the sun as the earth
Uranus	84.01 years	19.21	almost 20 times as far from the sun as the earth
Neptune	164.79 years	30.09	about 30 times as far from the sun as the earth
Pluto	285.50 years	39.75	about 40 times as far from the sun as the earth

The Third Law of Planetary Motion: Kepler calculated the distance of the planets from the sun by setting the earth's distance equal to 1.0. (note: The planets shown above are not to scale.)

The third law predicted the distance of a planet from the sun based on the time it takes to go around the sun. The value of the constant k could only be calculated if the distance from the sun of one planet was known. In Kepler's day, the distance of the earth or any other planet from the sun was not accurately known. For that reason, Kepler calculated the distances of the planets from the sun by setting the earth's distance equal to 1.0. From that, he calculated a scale model of the solar system.

The earth goes around the sun in one year. Saturn takes more than 29 years. Knowing this time, Kepler calculated that slow-moving Saturn was almost ten times as far from the sun as the earth. Mercury required only 88 days to complete its orbit. Speedy Mercury was only $4/10$ as far from the sun as the earth. For the first time, the vast size of the solar system became known.

Kepler's three laws of motion applied not only to the planets, but also to comets, satellites of planets, and even artificial satellites that orbit earth. Because his laws applied equally well to many different celestial objects, scientists began to think in terms of a few basic laws that explained all motion. Kepler began the process, still going on today, of trying to find basic, simple laws that govern how the universe works.

Kepler's discoveries showed that planets traveled faster when they were near the sun and more slowly when they were farther from the sun. What force could be acting on planets to make their speeds vary? No one knew.

Johannes Kepler (1571–1630) and Galileo (1564–1642) lived at about the same time. Their discoveries — Galileo's about motions on earth and Kepler's about motions in space — appeared to be unrelated. However, Isaac Newton showed that all objects in motion, whether in space or on earth, followed a simple set of rules.

Isaac was born on a cold Christmas day in 1642 outside the English town of Woolsthorpe. His father died before his birth. His mother was poor. When Isaac grew older he attended Cambridge University. He paid for his room

Newton discovered the law of gravity when observing an apple falling from his apple tree.

and meals by doing chores for his professors. He polished shoes, delivered messages, ran errands into town, and served the professors their dinners. Isaac studied theology and mathematics at Cambridge.

In 1665, terrible news interrupted Isaac's schooling. The Black Death — bubonic plague — struck London. As many as 10,000 people a month died. The Black Death spread to Cambridge itself. University officials closed the school for two terms. Students scattered from crowded cities and into the countryside where they would be safer from the epidemic.

Isaac thought about unsolved mysteries of science. One day while at his study table in an apple orchard, Isaac Newton began thinking about the discoveries of Galileo and Kepler. Galileo had shown that an apple would fall to earth in a straight line, but it constantly changed speed. Kepler had shown that the moon traveled at a nearly steady speed but constantly changed direction. It was as if the moon and the apple followed two different laws.

Isaac Newton realized that if the moon followed the rules of motion that Galileo discovered, it should travel in a straight line. The fact that they didn't showed that some force was at work. The force changed the direction the moon traveled.

Most scientists imagined that a whirlpool-like vortex pushed the moon in a curving motion. This imagined force shoved mostly behind the moon, but also turned it around an elliptical orbit.

Isaac Newton realized that rather than a force pushing the planet along, a force acted along a line connecting the moon to the earth. The force pulled the moon out of its straight-line path and around the earth. The force acted on the moon in the same way that the force of gravity acted on an apple — pulling it toward the center of the earth.

The apple was 4,000 miles from the center of the earth. The moon was 240,000 miles from the center of the earth. Isaac's calculations showed that the moon was 60 times farther away than the apple: 240,000/4,000 = 60. Would gravity acting on the moon be 60 times weaker?

Newton calculated the acceleration due to gravity of the moon. He found that the force acting on the moon was 3,600 times weaker than the force acting on the apple.

Isaac saw that 3,600 was 60 times 60 or 60 squared (60^2). This led him to the important conclusion that the force of gravity decreases by the square of the distance.

Actually, his results were not that clear-cut at first. For his calculations about the apple and the moon, Newton needed to know the size of the earth and the distance to the moon, but astronomers did not know these values exactly. His calculations showed that gravity was 3,630 times weaker. The answer was close to 3,600, but he decided not to publish his results because of that slight error.

When the Black Death ended, Isaac Newton returned to Cambridge, where he taught mathematics. Twenty years passed. A French expedition made a more accurate measure of the earth's size. Fresh calculations with the new information showed that his original idea was correct.

Center of Gravity

The jumper's body passes over the bar, but his center of gravity passes under the bar.

The center of mass is the point at which an object will balance. This point is also known as the center of gravity. The center of gravity of a yardstick is its balance point, a point located 18 inches from each end of the stick. Generally, if an object is symmetric and uniform in density, then its center of gravity and its geometric center coincide. The geometric center of a baseball is also its center of mass and center of gravity.

Controlling the center of gravity is important in modern transportation. For instance, the center of gravity of airplanes must not vary too greatly. In smaller airplanes that carry only a few people, the pilot must know the weights of his passengers, the weight of the luggage, and even the weight of the fuel that the plane carries. The pilot makes a calculation known as the weight and balance. Should the center of gravity fall too far forward or too far aft (to the back), then the luggage has to be moved or fuel pumped into different tanks. Otherwise, the plane would have a misplaced center of gravity and would be difficult to fly.

Ground transportation also requires attention to the center of gravity. A truck carrying a heavy load that rises above the cab has a high center of gravity. It is particularly apt to topple over should the truck turn too quickly. The truck is top heavy. The center of gravity lies above the geometric center.

The location of the center of gravity (or center of mass) determines the stability of an object. A coin set on edge has a high center of gravity and is unstable. The slightest touch will cause it to tip over. Once it falls over, the center of gravity is lower and the coin is stable. An object is most stable when its center of gravity is as low as possible.

An automobile with a lower center of gravity is more stable than one with a high center of gravity. One goal of automobile engineers is to design cars that do not tip over during sudden changes in direction such as evasive maneuvers to avoid hitting another vehicle.

The center of gravity can lie outside an object. A horseshoe has its center of gravity in the open space.

A successful high jumper has learned to control his or her center of gravity. When he goes over the bar, he moves his arms and legs, and bows his back so that at least half of the mass of his body is below the bar throughout the jump. As incredible as it may seem, the jumper's body passes over the bar, but his center of gravity passes under the bar.

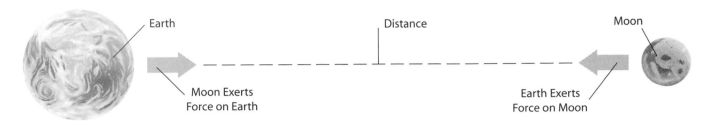

The gravitational force between the earth and the moon demonstrates Newton's Law of Gravity.

In 1687, Newton published *Principia*, in which he announced his three laws of motion and the law of gravity. Newton proved that all objects attract each other according to a simple equation. Sun, moon, planets, apples, and grains of sand are all subject to the law of gravity.

The law of gravity became Isaac Newton's best-known and most important discovery. Newton cautioned against thinking that the law of gravity alone could explain the universe. He said, "Gravity explains the motions of the planets, but it cannot explain who set the planets in motion. God governs all things, and knows all that is or can be done."

As the years passed, people came to understand the importance of his many discoveries. He was knighted, the first honor given to a scientist. When Isaac Newton died in 1727, he was buried in Westminster Abbey, the burial place for the nation's great leaders.

Despite his fame as a scientist, the Bible and not nature had been Isaac Newton's greatest passion. He devoted more time to Scripture than to science. He said, "I have a fundamental belief in the Bible as the Word of God, written by those who were inspired. I study the Bible daily."

Law of Gravity: Any two objects attract one another with a force of gravity that is directly proportional to the product of their masses and inversely proportional to the square of the distance separating them.

Distance is measured from the center of mass of the two objects. At the surface of the earth, a person is about 4,000 miles from the center of the earth. The distance from the center of the earth, and not the distance from the surface of the earth, is used in the law of gravity.

Distance and force of gravity are inversely related. If distance increases, the force of gravity grows weaker. The force decreases by the square of the distance. If the moon were twice as far away, then the gravitational attraction between it and the earth would be only one-fourth as great. If the moon were three times as far away, the gravitational attraction would be only one-ninth as great. This is described as an inverse square relationship.

As another example, suppose the mass of the earth did not change, but everything was squeezed into a smaller space so that the distance from the center of the earth to the surface was only 2,000 miles rather than 4,000 miles. A person on the surface of the earth would be only half as far from its center, so the person would weigh four times as much.

In fact, the force of gravity does change on earth because some locations are farther from the center of the earth. The highest mountain in the United States is Mount McKinley in Denali National Park, Alaska. It is 20,320 feet high. At its peak, a 170-pound mountain climber would weigh about six ounces less than at its base. The greater distance of the mountaintop from the center of the earth reduces the force of gravity.

The law of gravity states that the force of attraction between two bodies is directly proportional to the product of their masses. The reason masses are multiplied is clear when one thinks about Galileo's observation that all objects fall toward the earth at the same speed.

If a ten-pound steel ball and a one-pound steel ball are dropped, they will fall side by side. Yet, the massive ball has ten times as much inertia. It is ten times harder to get moving. However, according to the law of gravity, the force of attraction with the earth is ten times greater. The greater attractive force exactly overcomes the greater inertia.

Gravity acts between two objects, so both apple and earth attract one another. The apple exerts an extremely slight force of attraction for the earth. We normally say that the earth attracts an apple and causes it to fall. But according to the law of gravity, both earth and apple attract one another. The mass of the apple is very slight. Its gravity does not affect the earth in any way that can be measured.

The moon, however, does have enough mass to affect the earth. The moon doesn't merely circle the earth. Instead, earth and the moon circle around their combined center of mass. The earth has 81 times as much mass as the moon, so the center of mass is at a point about 3,000 miles from the center of the earth. (Divide 240,000 miles by 81 for the exact answer.) Because of the earth's greater mass, the center of mass is closer to the earth than to the moon.

Physicists write the law of gravity as an equation. Before we look at the law of gravity as an equation, we need to understand the concept of proportionality constant. Two

Artificial Satellites

In *Principia*, Newton's book about gravity, he suggested that an object could be put into orbit around the earth. One illustration in his book showed a powerful cannon on a mountaintop high above the atmosphere. If the cannon were powerful enough, it could shoot a cannonball all the way around the earth. The cannonball would be above the friction of the earth's atmosphere. It would continue circling the earth forever. Isaac Newton was the first to suggest that an artificial satellite could be put in orbit around the earth.

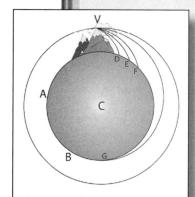

The first artificial satellite was put into orbit in 1957. Since then, satellites have been put in orbit to carry telephone, radio, and television signals, to observe the earth's weather, and to conduct scientific study.

One of the most interesting uses of satellites has been for a global positioning system (GPS.) A GPS receiver can locate your position within a few yards anywhere on earth. The system uses 24 satellites in precise orbits about 11,000 miles above the earth. The satellites transmit signals by radio waves back to earth. Part of the signal is a very precise time code. A GPS receiver on earth receives the signals from any 4 of the 24 satellites. It calculates the delay in the signal from each of the satellites, and can in this way pinpoint its own location.

GPS receiver

Because it works on land, sea, and in the air, hikers and hunters, boaters, fishermen, balloon pilots, and airplane pilots use GPS receivers. Computers can receive signals from GPS satellites to pinpoint the exact location of a car. Computer screens with built-in maps show drivers the best route. Ambulances and fire trucks can find their way to the scene of a disaster quickly and accurately.

quantities can be proportional without being equal. To make them equal, a proportionality constant must be used. A proportionality constant changes a proportion into equality. As an example, although feet and inches are related to one another, we cannot say that 6 feet equals 6 inches. Instead, we multiply 6 feet by the conversion factor of 12 inches per foot to get the number of inches: 6 ft = 12 in/ft × 6 ft = 72 in. The 12 in/ft is the conversion factor.

In the same way, if two quantities are proportional, then we can set them equal by using a conversion factor, called the proportionality constant.

In the case of the law of gravity, Isaac Newton used the letter G to stand for the gravitational proportionality constant. In symbols, the law of gravity can be written as:

$$F = G \frac{m_1 \times m_2}{d^2}$$

with F the force, G the gravitational constant, m_1 the mass of the first object, m_2 the mass of the second object, and d the distance separating their centers of mass.

Notice that the two masses are in the numerator. Force is directly proportional to the product of their masses. If either one is doubled in mass, force is doubled. If both are doubled in mass, force is four times as much.

Distance is in the denominator and it is squared. If distance is doubled, then the force of gravity is weaker by a factor of four.

The law of gravity is universal. Gravitational attraction exists between any two objects in the universe. Scientists have found that stars follow the law, as do small objects such as grains of sand.

In the 1600s, scientists realized that the stars are large, glowing objects like the sun, but very far away. Since then, scientists have wondered if stars had planets like those that orbit the sun. Stars are enormous, but they are so far away that most just look like points of light when viewed through even the most powerful telescopes. Planets would be even smaller and impossible to see directly. Despite the difficulty, astronomers have discovered planets orbiting

other suns. The first one was discovered in 1992. Since then, more than 100 planets have been detected in orbit around distant stars.

These hidden planets are revealed because of their gravitational effect on the stars they orbit. Stars travel through space, and powerful telescopes reveal this motion, but some stars are pulled from their straight course by objects orbiting them. Some of these unseen companions are very dim stars, but others are too small to be stars. They must be planets. As a planet orbits a star, the planet's gravity pulls the star first one way and then the other.

Jupiter is the largest planet in our solar system. The planet is large enough to cause the sun to wobble. If astronomers were on nearby stars, they would be able to see the back and forth motion caused to the sun as Jupiter goes around in its orbit.

The importance of Newton's discoveries is far-reaching. His three laws of motion and the law of gravity contained a summary of the discoveries in physics made in the previous 2,000 years.

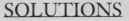

SOLUTIONS

1. Planets travel in elliptical, not circular, orbits.

2. All objects follow the three laws of motion.

3. A planet's gravity causes a star to wobble.

Newton's laws summarized discoveries about motion and gravity.

T F 1. During Kepler's time, most people believed the laws governing motions in the heavens differed from those for motions on earth.

A B C D 2. Kepler proved that planets traveled in orbits that were (A. circular B. elliptical C. parabolic D. straight-line).

A B 3. A planet travels (A. faster B. slower) when closer to the sun.

4. State the second law of planetary motion.

T F 5. Kepler's third law of motion reveals that planets farther from the sun take longer to orbit the sun.

A B 6. Isaac Newton built upon the discoveries of Galileo and (A. Aristotle B. Kepler).

T F 7. Isaac Newton came from a rich and powerful family.

T F 8. The direction the force of gravity acts on the moon is toward the center of the earth.

A B C 9. The moon is 60 times as far from the earth as an apple in a tree, so the force of earth's gravity on the moon is (A. 3,600 times weaker B. 60 times stronger C. 60 times weaker D. the same).

T F 10. The law of gravity applies only to the sun, moon, and planets.

A B 11. If the moon were twice as far away, gravitational attraction between Earth and the moon would be (A. one-half B. one-fourth) as great.

12. Force of gravitational attraction between two objects is directly proportional to the _____ of their masses and inversely proportional to the _____ of the distance separating them.

T F 13. Scientists have proven that our sun is the only star that has planets orbiting it.

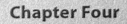
Simple Machines

For most of history, muscle power was the way work got done. In some places, windmills or water wheels ground grain or sawed wood, but muscles did the vast majority of tasks. Human muscles or the muscles of domestic animals such as horses or elephants did the manual labor. When muscles alone were not enough, then simple machines made the job easier. A simple machine can magnify a person's strength.

Simple machines include the lever, inclined plane, wheel and axle, and pulley. These devices are called simple machines to set them apart from more complicated machines such as a bicycle, electric motor or rocket engine.

A machine transmits a force from one place to another. A simple machine allows a person to overcome a resistance at one point by applying a force at some other point. The input force is the effort and the output force is the load. The load and effort are measured in force units —

PROBLEMS

1. Can a small force move a heavy load?

2. Do simple machines give something for nothing?

3. How did ancient Egyptians build the pyramids?

Can You Propose Solutions?

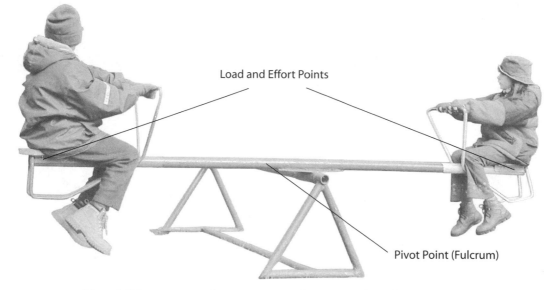

Load and Effort Points

Pivot Point (Fulcrum)

The children seesawing are using the principles of a simple lever.

pounds in the Customary System and newtons in the metric system.

A simple machine changes the amount of force needed to do a job or the direction the force is applied. A small effort can move a large load. For instance, a claw hammer allows a smaller force to pull out a reluctant nail. Force on the hammer handle is transmitted to the claw that extracts the nail. The force applied to the handle is the effort, and the resistance of the nail is the load. The force on the hammer handle is less than the force of the claw that extracts the nail.

Other arrangements of the same simple machine keep load and effort equal, but allow a person to apply the force in a more convenient direction. The pulley on a flagpole lets a person raise a flag by standing on the ground. The pulley changes direction of the applied force. Pulling down on the rope causes a flag to go up the pole.

The Greek scientist Archimedes investigated simple machines such as levers, inclined planes, and pulleys. He once said, "Give me a place to stand and a long enough lever, and I can move the world." Although such a test could not be done, he did demonstrate the usefulness of simple machines. With a series of pulleys, he single-handedly dragged a fully loaded barge onto shore.

Weight is the force of gravity, and many simple machines allow a person to apply a force to move a heavy weight more easily. Pulleys allowed Archimedes, with his limited strength, to pull a barge that weighs several tons up on the shore.

Archimedes expressed the usefulness of simple machines in scientific terms. He developed the idea of mechanical advantage. Archimedes described the mechanical advantage as the ratio of load to effort.

For instance, if you press down on a pry bar (a type of lever) with a force of 30 pounds and succeed in prying up a 600-pound load, then the mechanical advantage is 600 pounds divided by 30 pounds, or 20. Mechanical advantage written as an equation is M.A. = load/effort. Mechanical advantage is a number without units because the units divide out. However, the load and effort must be measured in the same units, usually pounds in the Customary System and newtons in the metric system.

A few pounds of force at one end of the lever exert a much greater force at the other end of the lever. Archimedes also realized that you do not get something for nothing. His experiments showed that a few pounds of effort had to be applied over a much greater distance. The reduced force came at the expense of greater distance. For example, when a claw hammer extracts a nail, the distance the handle moves is greater than the distance the nail moves.

Archimedes

Unlike Aristotle, who lived 50 years earlier, Archimedes took a hands-on approach to science. Archimedes was born in 287 B.C. Despite living more than 2,000 years ago, he approached science much as modern scientists do. He did experiments and summarized results with mathematical precision. He built inventions with his own hands.

He studied at the great university at Alexandria, Egypt, and then returned to his home in the port city of Syracuse on the island of Sicily. The king of Syracuse paid him a salary to make scientific discoveries that helped the city. Archimedes became the foremost scientist of ancient times. He also made important discoveries in mathematics.

He was one of the first scientists to understand the concept that the books must balance. He realized that simple machines did not give something for nothing. The reduced force came at the expense of applying the force through a greater distance. Overall, the same amount of energy had to be expended.

Archimedes

Today, scientists are especially careful to account for any missing mass, momentum, or energy. Nuclear scientists are especially vigilant because keeping the books in balance is the main way they identify new subatomic particles. Should some conserved quantity go missing, they know to look for an invisible particle that carried away the missing quantity. Several subatomic particles have been discovered in this way.

Levers are found all around us today. The ring that pops the tab on a soft drink can is a lever. Wheelbarrows, tweezers, baseball bats, fishing rods, and many tools are levers.

The pivot point of a lever is called the fulcrum. A simple playground seesaw is an example of a lever. The pivot point is near the middle and children on each end occupy the load and effort points. Should one child be heavier than the other, he would need to sit closer to the pivot point. Otherwise the seesaw would not balance.

Levers differ depending on the position of the fulcrum, load, and effort. Usually, a lever is shown with the fulcrum in the middle. But a lever can also have the load in the middle and the fulcrum at one end, and the effort at the other end. A nutcracker has the load (the nut to be cracked) between the fulcrum and effort. A wheelbarrow is another example with the fulcrum at one end and the load between fulcrum and effort. The wheel of the barrel is the fulcrum, the contents of the barrel are the load, and the effort is at the handles.

A third arrangement of a lever has the effort in the middle, the fulcrum at one end,

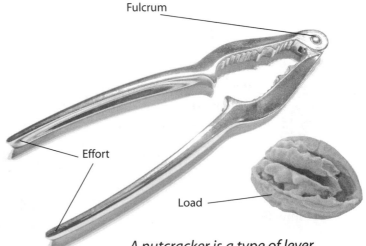

Fulcrum

Effort

Load

A nutcracker is a type of lever.

and the load at the other end. A fishing pole is an example of this type of lever. People who go deep-sea fishing push the base of the pole into a holder on a belt around their waist. The holder is the fulcrum, or pivot point, for the fishing pole. The fish is the load and tugs on the line at the end of the pole. The fisherman applies his effort by holding the pole near the reel up a ways from the fulcrum.

During his experiments with levers, Archimedes discovered another way to measure mechanical advantage. He calculated mechanical advantage by measuring the distance from the fulcrum to the load and from the fulcrum to the effort. The mechanical advantage of a lever is the length of the effort arm divided by the length of the load arm: M.A. = (effort arm)/(load arm).

A lever with equal lengths for effort arm and load arm has a mechanical advantage of one. For instance, most playground seesaws have places for children to sit equally spaced from the fulcrum that is in the middle. Because the load arm and effort arm are equal, the mechanical advantage is one. If one child is much heavier than the other, then he or she must move closer to the center to give the other child a mechanical advantage greater than 1.0.

A lever with the effort arm longer than the load arm has a mechanical advantage greater than 1.0. The pull-tab to open a pop-top soda can is an example of a lever with the effort arm longer than the load arm. The fulcrum is a small metal brad. From the end of the ring to the brad is about 20 millimeters. From the brad to the part that presses against the can is about 4 millimeters. The mechanical advantage is 5.0: M.A. = effort arm/load arm = 20 mm/ 4 mm = 5.0.

A lever with the effort arm shorter than the load arm has a mechanical advantage of less than 1.0. In the case of a fly fishing rod, the effort is applied near the fulcrum, but the weight of the lure is at the end of the pole. A force greater than the weight of the lure must be applied. But the lure moves through

Ramps and the Pyramids

The Great Pyramid of Giza

The ancient Egyptians built the pyramids with the aid of temporary ramps. The largest pyramid, the Great Pyramid of Giza, forms a nearly perfect square 756 feet on a side and rises to a height of about 480 feet. Scientists estimate that it contains about 2,300,000 blocks, each weighing about 5,500 pounds.

The large blocks were pulled up ramps. A long and gentle slope makes it easier to move heavy building stones. Egyptian workers reduced the effort even more by rolling the blocks on round poles and reduced the friction by using butter as a lubricant. Once they completed the pyramid, they removed the ramps.

a greater distance than the arm pulling on the pole. The fly fisherman trades the lower mechanical advantage to gain speed. A small movement of the pole flips the lure away at a faster speed.

A ramp is an example of an inclined plane, another type of simple machine. The idea of making a job easier by using a ramp rather than lifting a load directly goes far back in history. Scholars believe the Tower of Babel, mentioned in Genesis 11:9, had a long, spiraling ramp. People carried loads to the top by walking around and around the ramp.

Today, roads are engineered to reduce the angle at which vehicles must climb up a mountain. Trucks with heavy loads can travel easier on roads with low grades. The grade is a measure of how quickly a roadbed rises or falls. Most roads have a grade of less than 6 percent. For every 100 feet of travel, a road rises 6 feet.

Making a longer approach lowers the effort of getting to the top. The mechanical advantage of an inclined plane is equal to the run along the ramp divided by the rise of the ramp: M.A. = ramp length/ramp height = run/rise. The equation is another way of showing that the mechanical advantage is equal to the distance the effort must be applied compared to the distance the load is raised. A road that rises 6 feet for every 100 feet has a mechanical advantage of 16.7. M.A. = ramp length/ramp height = 100 ft/6 ft = 16.7.

Many restaurants and other places of business have installed handicapped ramps. The purpose of the ramps is not only to replace steps but also reduce the effort that it takes to roll a wheelchair up the ramp. A handicap ramp should not rise more than one inch for every foot (12 inches) that it runs. A handicap ramp 36 feet long that rises three feet has a mechanical advantage of 12. M.A. = run/rise = 36 ft/3 ft = 12. If a wheelchair and the person in the wheelchair weigh a total of 180 pounds, then an effort of only 15 pounds is needed to roll up the ramp. (Divide 180 by 12.)

The third type of simple machine is a wheel and axle. An early use of a wheel and axle was to raise a bucket of water from a well. A rope tied to the axle passed down to the bucket. Turning the wheel wound the rope around the axle and raised the bucket of water. A windlass, a type of wheel and axle, was used to raise a castle's drawbridge. For each turn of the axle, the wheel turns once, too. The axle is usually smaller than the wheel, so it is easier to turn the wheel than to turn the axle directly. The wheel of a windlass

A windlass, a type of wheel and axle, is used to raise a bucket full of water from a well.

had handles that gave even more mechanical advantage.

The distance the wheel turns compared to the distance the axle turns gives the mechanical advantage. The distance around a circle, the circumference, is proportional to the diameter of the circle. The mechanical advantage of a wheel and axle is found by dividing the diameter of the wheel by the diameter of the axle.

A screwdriver is an example of a wheel and axle. The handle is the wheel and the shaft is the axle. A screwdriver with a handle 25 millimeters in diameter and a shaft five millimeters in diameter has a mechanical advantage of five. M.A. = (wheel diameter)/(axle diameter) = 25 mm/5 mm = 5.0.

Sometimes the effort is applied to the axle. For example, the rear wheel of a bicycle is a wheel and axle. The axle has gears for the bicycle chain. As a person pedals, each turn of the small axle gives a much greater travel distance of the larger wheel.

A pulley is the fourth type of simple machine. A pulley has a rope that passes through one or more wheels. For pulleys, one way to measure mechanical advantage is to see how far the load moves compared to how far the effort is exerted.

A pulley that raises a flag to the top of a flagpole has a mechanical advantage of one. The rope goes up to the top of the flagpole, around a wheel, and then back down to the flag. A person who raises the flag pulls one foot of rope for each foot the flag raises. To raise the flag 20 feet, then 20 feet of rope must pass through the hands of the person who raises the flag. Because the distances are equal, the mechanical advantage is 1.0: M.A. = effort distance/load distance = 20 ft/20 ft = 1.0.

Rather than being fixed at the top, a pulley can have a hook that is attached to the load. A person on top of a building who pulls up a bucket of sealing tar for the roof uses a pulley of this type. Fasten the rope to a hook in the pulley that is fastened to the bucket. The rope goes from there up through the wheel of the roof pulley back down through the wheel of the bucket pulley and back up through another wheel of the roof pulley and is pulled by the worker. Three lengths of rope support the load. For a roof 30 feet high, a total of 90 feet of rope is pulled through the worker's hands by the time the bucket gets to the top. The mechanical advantage is three. M.A. = effort distance/load distance = 90 feet/30 feet = 3.0.

How does the flagpole pulley differ from the bucket pulley? Notice that the pulley at the top of the flagpole remains at the top of the flagpole. It does not move, but the pulley with the load attached moves to the top of the roof. Another way to calculate the mechanical

Here is a single pulley used on a sail boat.

advantage of a pulley is by counting the number of ropes that move the load. In the bucket example, three ropes support the bucket. The load is due to the force of gravity. Each rope supports one-third of the total load. The mechanical advantage is three.

Pulleys are used today for many jobs. Venetian blinds are raised and lowered with a pulley system. Some garage door openers raise the door with a pulley. Car repair shops use pulleys to lift heavy engines from automobiles. Window washers raise and lower scaffoldings by pulleys.

When a large mechanical advantage is desirable, a block and tackle is used. The pulleys are put together in groups called blocks. One block is fixed in place overhead, and the lower block has a hook to attach to the load. The rope runs back and forth through each of the wheels in the overhead and lower blocks. The lower block rises with the load. Block and tackles for doing heavy lifting use steel cables or chains rather than ropes. A crane, for instance, lifts heavy loads to the top of buildings under construction with block and tackle that use steel cables.

The mechanical advantage of a block and tackle depends on the number of ropes, cables, or chains that move the load. If eight ropes hold the load, then the mechanical advantage is eight. A 400-pound engine can be moved from a car with 50 pounds of effort. (Divide 400 pounds by the mechanical advantage of eight.)

The four basic simple machines are lever, inclined plane, wheel and axle, and pulley. Modifying one of the four simple machines or combining them makes other

Painters use a floating pulley held by three ropes.

simple machines. A wedge for splitting wood is two inclined planes put back to back. A nail has a point made of four surfaces that come to a point. Each surface is an inclined plane. Hammering a nail into a block of wood is easier because the hole in the wood starts small and gets bigger. A screw has a similar advantage. A screw is an inclined plane wrapped around a cylinder.

Tweezers are two levers that have a single fulcrum at the end. Scissors are two levers that share a single fulcrum near the middle. In addition, the cutting edges of scissors are types of inclined planes. A bicycle is made almost entirely of combinations of simple machines.

The actual mechanical advantage of any simple machine is given by the equation first proposed by Archimedes:

$$\text{Actual M.A.} = \text{effort} / \text{load}$$

Work is defined as the force times the distance the force is applied: work = force × distance. If friction is ignored, the work (effort times distance it is applied) going into a simple machine equals the work (load times distance the load moves) produced by the simple machine.

As machines become more complex, friction robs some of the mechanical advantage. Friction changes some energy into heat that does no useful work in moving the load. To completely remove friction is virtually impossible. This means that the theoretical mechanical advantage and the actual mechanical advantage will not agree. The work put into the simple machine is greater than the work produced by the simple machine.

For a machine with high efficiency, most of the work going into the machine ends up doing the job for which the machine was designed. The efficiency of a machine is the work input compared to the work output expressed as a percent. As an equation,

$$\text{efficiency} = \frac{(\text{work output})}{(\text{work input})} \times 100\%$$

A machine with no friction or other hindrance to its movement would have an efficiency of 100 percent. Simple machines do transmit force without much loss. A lever, for instance, has efficiency very close to 100 percent. A block and tackle is not as efficient as a lever. A block and tackle has a large number of pulleys that increase friction and opportunities for the rope to bind. Generally, the more complex a machine becomes and the more moving parts it has, the less efficient it is. An automobile or other large vehicle is less efficient than a simple machine.

Long ago, some people thought simple machines gave them something for nothing. Archimedes recognized that the reduced force came at the expense of applying it over a greater distance. Scientists are very suspicious when they appear to get something for nothing.

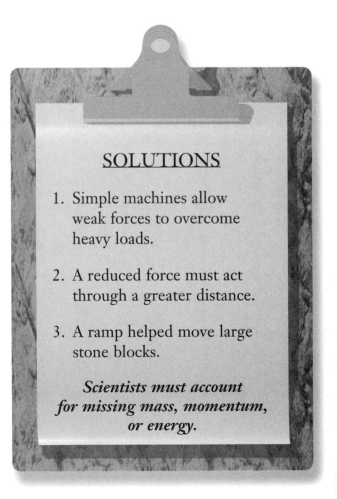

SOLUTIONS

1. Simple machines allow weak forces to overcome heavy loads.

2. A reduced force must act through a greater distance.

3. A ramp helped move large stone blocks.

Scientists must account for missing mass, momentum, or energy.

1. A simple machine changes the amount of _____ needed to do a job or the direction the _____ is applied. (same word)

A B C D 2. The Greek who said, "Give me a place to stand and a long enough lever, and I can move the world" was (A. Archimedes   B. Aristotle   C. Eratosthenes   D. Ptolemy).

A B 3. Mechanical advantage is found by dividing load by (A. effort B. gravity).

A B C D 4. The tab on a soft drink can is an example of (A. an inclined plane B. a lever   C. a pulley   D. a wheel and axle).

T F 5. The pivot point (fulcrum) of a lever must be located in the middle.

A B 6. If a load is moved closer to the fulcrum than the effort, the effort required to move the load will be (A. increased   B. reduced).

7. The Grand Canyon is about one mile deep, and the most popular trail out of the canyon is nine miles long; the mechanical advantage of the trail is _____.

A B C D 8. A screwdriver is an example of (A. a pulley   B. a ramp C. a wheel and axle   D. an inclined plane).

T F 9. A screw is an inclined plane wrapped around a cylinder.

T F 10. Because of friction, the work produced by a simple machine is greater than the work put into a simple machine.

A B 11. The one that is likely to be the least efficient is a (A. simple machine B. 18 wheeler truck).

A B 12. A machine with no friction or other hindrance to its movement would have an efficiency of (A. zero   B. 100) percent.

5

Energy

The human body has several senses. The five we are most aware of are vision, hearing, touch, taste, and smell. Three of the senses are used primarily to give us information about matter. Everything we touch, taste, and smell is an example of matter. Matter has mass and takes up space.

The other two senses are used primarily to give us information about two forms of energy. Our eyes give us information about light energy and our ears detect sound energy.

Although matter and energy make up the physical universe, scientists did not become aware of the properties of energy or how best to describe it until the early 1800s. The word energy was first used as a literary term to mean a powerfully written piece or speech. In 1807, Thomas Young, an English scientist, proposed the term for anything that was capable of putting an object in motion. Energy can put matter in motion.

PROBLEMS

1. How is an electric battery like water behind a dam?

2. How is a watt like a horsepower?

3. Does a moving object have energy?

Can You Propose Solutions?

In the 1800s, mechanical energy and heat energy were forms of energy in daily use. Over the years, scientists found other forms of energy — chemical, electrical, magnetic, solar, atomic, and nuclear.

Inventors learned how to change one form of energy into another. For instance, at a power plant, coal is burned to produce heat that boils water, steam turns a turbine, the mechanical action of the spinning turbine generates electricity, and the electricity can then be sent over wires and used in the home. It can be converted back into heat to brown toast or heat a room.

Scientists also learned that energy could be stored. Stored energy is called potential energy. Water behind a dam has potential energy. It is not in use, but can do work when released from the dam. A battery has potential chemical energy. Once the circuit is complete, the battery produces electricity that can then be used to start a car or power a cell phone.

Scientists defined energy as the ability to do work. According to the second law of motion, a force is necessary to put an object in motion. Scientists defined work as the force that acts on an object times the distance through which the force acts. The equation for work is $E = f \times d$, with E the work, f the force and d the distance. The letter E is used for work because W is often used for weight. Besides, E can be thought of as meaning energy as well. The two terms, energy and work, are closely related.

Work moves energy from one object to another. A battery in a radio transfers its energy to the speakers that then produce sound. Sound is caused by waves in air, so the energy is transferred from the battery to the air. When the energy transfer ceases, then no more work is being done. When a soccer player kicks a ball, he does work because he transfers energy from his foot to the ball. Although scientists make a distinction

A coal burning power plant changes heat into electricity.

between energy and work, they often use the two words interchangeably.

Work transfers energy from one place to another. Suppose a one-pound book is lifted from the floor to the top of a table that is three feet above the floor. Energy is transferred from the person doing the lifting to the book that is being raised. On the table the book has more potential energy than it did on the floor. The energy would be released if the book fell from the table.

In the English system, the unit for work is foot-pound. In the example of the one-pound book that is lifted three feet, the work is three foot-pounds: $E = f \times d = 1 \text{ lb} \times 3 \text{ ft} = 3 \text{ ft-lb}$.

In the metric system, the unit for work is the joule. It is the action of one newton of force through one meter of distance.

The joule is named in honor of James Prescott Joule, an Englishman who developed ways to measure different forms of energy. In the 1840s, the time when Joule lived, engineers

A completed circuit powers a cell phone.

measured mechanical energy in foot-pounds, but chemists measured heat energy in British thermal units (Btu). One Btu was the heat energy that would raise the temperature of one pound of water one degree Fahrenheit.

How many Btus are needed to make a foot-pound? In the 1840s, no one knew how to compare the two units.

Joule developed several sensitive experiments to learn the conversion factor of mechanical energy to heat energy. He made thermometers that could measure slight changes in temperature. For instance, one of his thermometers could measure the change in room temperature caused by a person's body heat.

He put a sensitive thermometer in an insulated container and stirred the water by letting a falling weight attached to a pulley turn paddles. He

James Prescott Joule

calculated the mechanical energy given to the water by the falling weight. The stirring of the water caused it to increase in temperature, which he measured with his precise thermometer. He found that 772 foot-pounds of work were needed to raise the temperature of one pound of water one degree Fahrenheit.

One Btu equals 772 foot-pounds.

In other words, Joule found how mechanical energy due to motion compares to heat energy.

In the metric system, heat is measured with the calorie. A calorie is the heat energy needed to raise the temperature of one gram of water one degree Celsius. (This is the scientific calorie. The calorie used in the nutritional labels on containers of food is known as the big calorie. It is equal to 1,000 scientific calories.) In the metric system, a calorie is equal to a little more than four joules. One Btu is 1,055 joules.

By the way, memorizing conversion factors is convenient if you work with them often. For instance, most people have memorized that 12 inches make a foot and that 16 ounces make a pound. However, it is more profitable to first understand how to apply concepts of physics than to memorize conversion factors or equations.

As an example of thinking about the scientific meaning of work, suppose a student is moving a heavy desk and pushes against it with a force of 40 pounds. The stubborn desk refuses to move. The student doubles his effort and continues to shove against the desk for five minutes before giving up. How much work is done? The equation for work is

A soccer player transfers energy from his foot to the ball.

W = F × d. The desk does not move, so the distance is zero. Force, no matter how great, times zero is still zero. The desk does not move, so no work has been done in the scientific sense.

In calculating work, distance must be in the direction that the force is applied. For instance, suppose a student that weighs 90 pounds climbs a vertical ladder to the top of a building that is 30 feet high. The work is 2,700 foot pounds: $E = f \times d = 90 \text{ lb} \times 30 \text{ ft} = 2{,}700 \text{ ft-lbs}$. Another student of the same weight walks along a 200-foot ramp to the top of the building. Although the second student travels a greater distance, he has done the same amount of work. His effort against gravity is the vertical distance he has walked, not the horizontal distance. He also does the same amount of work whether he does it quickly or slowly. Time is not part of the equation for work.

Power measures how quickly energy is supplied. Work can be done slowly or it can be done quickly. The faster work is done, the faster energy must be supplied.

The speed at which work is done is often important. For instance, two dragsters line up beside one another to speed down a quarter-mile track. When the light turns green, they thunder away and spectators watch to see which one crosses the finish line first. Getting up to speed quickly is as important as the top speed. It is possible for two dragsters to cross the finish line at the same speed, but one gets there first because it got up to speed more quickly. His engine had more power.

Power is how quickly work is done. As an equation, power is $P = E/t$, with P the power, E the work, and t the time.

The standard unit of power in the Customary system is the horsepower (hp.) The idea of a horsepower was invented by James Watt. He built the first practical steam engines in the late 1700s. Most work at that time was done by muscle power — either that of humans or animals such as horses.

As a selling point, Watt compared the power of his steam engines to a horse. First, he decided it should be a job that the horse could do all day long and not become too tired. He measured the load a strong horse

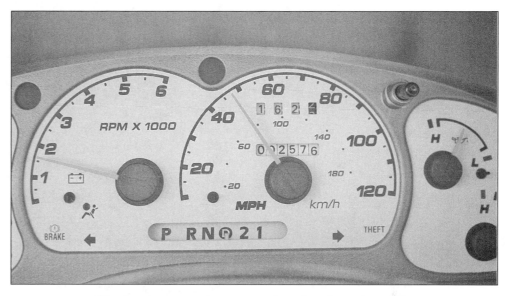

The horsepower that an engine develops depends upon how fast the engine runs.

could lift with continuous effort and found it to be 22,000 foot-pounds per minute. To avoid argument that some horses might be stronger, he set one horsepower equal to 33,000 foot-pounds of work per minute, or 550 foot-pounds per second. Watts most popular machine was a 20 horsepower model.

Today, automobile engines in the United States are rated in horsepower. Three different versions of horsepower are used. One is the horsepower developed by the pressure in the cylinders of the engine. But in going from the engine to the wheels, some of this power is lost because of friction. The horsepower that reaches the wheels is called brake or shaft horsepower.

Engines are also given a horsepower number based on the horsepower they develop when running at their most efficient setting. This is less than when going at top speed. For instance, an engine of a small airplane may develop 120 hp when going at its top rate and turns the propeller at 2,800 revolutions per minute. But it may produce only 100 hp at normal cruise speed when it turns the propeller at 2,200 revolutions per minute.

Like engines, human beings can develop power that varies in how long it is maintained. Suppose a student who weighs 90 pounds runs up a flight of stairs 20 feet high in 8 seconds. What is the power in foot-pounds per second (ft-lbs/sec) and horsepower (hp)? First calculate the work: $E = f \times d = 90$ lbs $\times 20$ ft $= 1,800$ ft-lbs. Then divide work by time to give power: $P = E/t = (1,800 \text{ ft-lbs})/8$ sec $= 225$ ft-lbs/sec. A full horsepower is 550 ft-lb/sec, so 225 ft-lb/sec is ½ of a horsepower.

When a healthy adult goes full out, he can produce about 1.0 horsepower, but only for a short time. A strong, healthy adult who does heavy work all day long generates about ⅛ horsepower at a steady pace.

On June 12, 1980, Bryan Allen became the first to pedal a human powered aircraft, called the *Gossamer Albatross*, across the English Channel. The 22-mile journey from England to the coast of France took 2 hours and 49 minutes. Bryan Allen's muscles had to produce almost ½ horsepower throughout the trip.

Kites flying in the wind exhibit a form of kinetic energy.

In the metric system, the unit for power is watt (named after James Watt, of course). A watt is one joule of work per second. A horsepower is 746 watts.

As the early scientists developed an understanding of energy and power, they also learned about the energy possessed by moving objects.

Kinetic energy is the energy of motion. Kinetic is from a Greek word meaning to move. Kinetic energy takes many forms — a spinning turbine, an arrow in flight, a football player rushing the quarterback, water flowing in a stream, or wind holding up a kite.

The amount of kinetic energy depends on two properties, mass of the object and its speed.

For instance, suppose a bobsled has two riders. At the end of the run down the icy course, the bobsled crosses the finish line at a certain speed, say 30 miles per hour. At the finish line with that speed, the bobsled has a certain amount of kinetic energy — energy due to the combined mass of bobsled and riders and their speed. Suppose now that the two-person bobsled is replaced with a more massive one that has four riders. If the second sled and riders have a total mass that is double the first bobsled, and it crosses the finish line at the same speed, then it has twice the kinetic energy.

When all other quantities are equal, a doubling of mass doubles the kinetic energy of a moving object. If you triple the mass, then you triple the kinetic energy. Physicists say that kinetic energy is directly proportional to mass.

Kinetic energy and speed are also directly related. As the speed increases, so does the kinetic energy. But a change in velocity changes kinetic energy by a greater amount than a corresponding change in mass. The energy of a moving object is directly related to the square of the velocity. For instance, if the two-person bobsled manages to get to a speed of 60 miles per hour, then it has four times as much kinetic energy as it did at 30 miles per hour. Doubling the speed quadruples the kinetic energy.

The equation for kinetic energy is K.E. = $\frac{1}{2} \times m \times v^2$ with K.E. the kinetic energy, m the mass and v the velocity. This equation shows that kinetic energy is equal to one-half of the product of the mass and velocity squared.

The velocity squared shows that kinetic energy increases very rapidly with increasing speed. A car going 45 miles per hour has well over double the kinetic energy of a car with the same mass going 30 miles an hour. Thirty squared is 900 but 45 squared is 2,025. Dividing 2,025 by 900 shows that the faster car has 2.25 the kinetic energy of the slower car.

Think about it: a curve that can be taken safely at 30 miles per hour is four times as difficult to go around at 60 miles per hour, and nine times more difficult to negotiate at 90 miles per hour.

For More Study—Equation for Kinetic Energy

The equation for kinetic energy can be derived by combining the equation for distance: $d = \frac{1}{2} a \times t^2$, the equation for velocity, $v = a \times t$ (see chapter 1: Motion), and the force equation, $f = m \times a$ (see chapter 2: Laws of Motion). The second law of motion says that acceleration is directly proportional to the force and inversely proportional to the mass, $a = F/m$. The second law is often rewritten as the force equation. Force is equal to mass times acceleration: $F = m \times a$.

$F = m \times a$	force equation
$F \times d = m \times a \times d$	multiply both sides by distance
$K.E. = m \times a \times d$	$F \times d$ is the definition of work (energy)
$K.E. = m \times a \times (\frac{1}{2} a \times t^2)$	replace distance with $\frac{1}{2} a \times t^2$
$K.E = \frac{1}{2}m \times (a \times t)^2$	regroup
$K.E. = \frac{1}{2} m \times v^2$	replace $a \times t$ with v

Which has more kinetic energy, a 41-kg (about 90 pounds) student who is walking at 1.5 m/sec (about 3.0 mi/hr) or a 1.0 kg (about 2.2 lb) peregrine falcon flying at 90 m/sec (about 200 miles per hour.)

K.E. student = $\frac{1}{2} m \times v^2$
K.E. student = $\frac{1}{2}$ 41 kg $\times$ (1.5 m/sec)^2
K.E. student = 20.5 kg $\times$ 2.25 m^2/sec^2
K.E. student = 46 kg m^2/sec^2 or 46 joules

K.E. falcon = $\frac{1}{2} m \times v^2$
K.E. falcon = $\frac{1}{2}$ 1.0 kg $\times$ (90 m/sec)^2
K.E. falcon = 0.500 kg $\times$ 8,100 m^2/sec^2
K.E. falcon = 4,050 kg m^2/sec^2 or 4,050 joules

The falcon has about twice as much kinetic energy as the student: 46/4,050 = 1/88

Because of a car's kinetic energy due to its velocity, a curve that can be taken safely at 30 miles per hour is four times as difficult to go around at 60 miles per hour.

Imagine the kinetic energy that is contained in a race car that is going 200 miles per hour. Engineers design the car to protect the driver during a collision. Around the driver is a strong cage, but the rest of the car is designed to come apart. During a collision, metal panels that make the skin of the car separate, wheels come off, and other parts fly through the air. The flying parts carry away some kinetic energy. The cage with the driver stops without having to lose as much kinetic energy.

A spacecraft in orbit around the earth travels at about 17,500 miles per hour. When a space shuttle returns to earth, it must safely deplete its great kinetic energy. The space shuttle is lined with special heat tiles that glow as the kinetic energy of the shuttle is changed to heat energy from the friction with the atmosphere.

Energy can also be contained in an object when it is not moving. This energy is known as potential energy. Potential energy has been used from the earliest days. A drawn bow has potential energy. Once it is released, the potential energy of the bow is given to the arrow as kinetic energy. Gristmills for grinding grain into flour used the stored energy of water behind a dam.

Clocks and watches use stored energy to keep them running. Pendulum clocks, known as grandfather clocks, use a falling weight to keep the pendulum moving back and forth.

Old-fashioned alarm clocks use a wound spring to provide energy to the clock from one day to the next and to ring the alarm. Today, batteries run clocks, radios, cell phones, and numerous other devices. The batteries have

If masses of two objects are identical, the faster one has the greater kinetic energy.

For More Study —
Equation for Gravitational Potential Energy

The equation for gravitational potential energy, P.E. = m × g × h, is a combination of two other equations, the force equation and the definition of work.

For gravitational potential energy, the acceleration, a, is equal to the acceleration due to gravity, g. The force equation can be written as F = m × g.

Work is defined as the force times the distance the force is applied: E = F × d. In the case of gravitational potential energy, distance, d, is equal to height, and work is equal to potential energy. The equation E = F × d can be written as P.E. = F × h.

Combining the two equations gives the equation for gravitational potential energy:

E = F × d	definition of energy
P.E. = F × h	replace E with P.E. and d with h
P.E. = (m × a) × h	replace F with m × a
P.E. = m × g × h	replace a with g

In the metric system, work and potential energy are measured in joules, mass is measured in kilograms, acceleration of gravity is 9.81 m/sec^2, and height is measured in meters. What is the gravitational potential energy of four kilograms of water at the top of a 60-meter high dam?

P.E. = m × g × h
P.E. = 4 kg × 9.81 m/sec^2 × 60 m
P.E. = 2,350 kg m^2/sec^2 round 2,354.4
                                                        to 2,350
P.E. = 2,350 joules

The weight of an object is defined as the force produced by gravity, so weight is

A turbine generates electricity.

a type of force. The force equation, F = m × a, is also the weight equation with weight, W, replacing force, F, and the acceleration due to gravity, g, replacing acceleration, a. W = m × g.

In the Customary system, a pound is a measure of weight rather than mass. An object that weighs eight pounds presses down with a force of eight pounds. When calculating the gravitational potential energy in the Customary system, the equation is P.E. = W × h, with W the weight in pounds and h the height in feet.

What is the gravitational potential energy of each gallon of water that can flow over a dam 200 feet high? A gallon of water weighs eight pounds.

P.E. = W × h
P.E. = 8 lbs × 200 ft
P.E. = 1,600 ft-lbs

Dams use gravitational potential energy to generate electricity.

potential energy that is converted into electrical energy to power the devices.

Potential energy is stored energy. Potential energy has the ability to do work. It is measured in the same units as work — foot-pounds in the Customary system and joules in the metric system.

Gravitational potential energy is one of the most common forms of potential energy. The United States has an extensive system of dams that use gravitational potential energy to generate electricity. Water released from the dam falls to a lower level. The potential energy changes to kinetic energy. The rushing water spins a propeller-like device called a turbine that generates electricity.

The advantage of dams is that the water stores the energy until it is needed. During low demand for electricity, the flow of water is reduced and the excess water remains behind the dam. In time of high demand, more water is released.

Gravitational potential energy is given by the equation P.E. = m $\times$ g $\times$ h, with P.E. the potential energy, m the mass, g the acceleration due to gravity, and h the height. The acceleration due to gravity cannot be changed, so the two quantities that can be controlled are mass and height.

The equation P.E. = m $\times$ g $\times$ h shows that potential energy is directly proportion to both mass and height. For potential energy of water in a lake to double, then the amount of water behind the dam has to double, or the dam has to be made higher to double the distance that the water falls.

A bungee jumper is a good example of the relationship between potential energy and kinetic energy. The jumper stands on a high place such as a bridge and throws himself clear of the bridge. As he leaps away, he has potential energy because of his height above the ground. As he falls, he gains kinetic energy at the expense of potential energy. When the slack in the bungee is taken out, all of his potential energy has been changed into kinetic energy.

Now, the bungee begins absorbing the kinetic energy. The rubber of the bungee stretches and gains potential energy as it slows the jumper. At the bottom of the drop, the bungee is stretched as far as it will go. For a moment the jumper comes to a stop. He no longer has kinetic energy. Then the potential energy in the bungee begins pulling him back

Heat and Kinetic Energy

Native Americans and Australian Aborigines made fire with fire drills.

One way to demonstrate how kinetic energy can change into heat energy is to drive a nail with a hammer into a piece of hard wood. First, feel the head of the nail and notice its temperature. Then strike it several times and drive it into the hard wood. Feel the head of the nail again. It will be noticeably warmer. If the nail is difficult to drive and takes several blows with the hammer, even the head of the hammer may become warmer, too.

As an electric drill spins into wood, it also produces heat. Sometimes smoke will curl up around the drill. If the wood is dry and is hard enough to resist the drill, then the sawdust produced by the drill will catch fire.

Starting a fire by rubbing two pieces of wood together is possible, but requires both skill and preparation. The stick must be of a hard wood such as hickory. It should have a blunt point at one end. The block of wood should be a soft wood such as pine with a small depression in it for the blunt end of the stick. Place a fine, dry combustible material on the block around where the stick meets the block. Spin the stick rapidly back and forth between the palms of your hand while also pushing down.

When the combustible material starts to smoke, gently slide the glowing embers into a handful of dry grass or very fine wood shavings. Some people blow to encourage the flames, but if your breath is heavy with moisture, this will cool down the fire. It is better to gently fan the glowing embers with your hand or a sheet of cardboard.

Usually, such a fire-making attempt results in sore hands with blisters on the palms — but no fire. A better way is with a fire drill. A fire drill has a cord looped around the stick and held with a bow. The bow is sawed rapidly back and forth, which causes the stick to spin. Another block of wood is held by the other hand to press down on the stick. The upper block can be lightly lubricated. Friction changes the motion of the stick against the lower block into heat.

Native Americans and Australian Aborigines made fire in this way. Usually, when they found fire sticks that worked well, they kept them to use time and again. They could generate a fire with a fire drill in less than two minutes.

Potential energy changes to kinetic energy as the bungee jumper falls.

up again. Once again the jumper gains kinetic energy at the expense of potential energy.

After bouncing up and down a few times, the jumper comes to a stop. Neither potential energy nor kinetic energy remains. What happened to the energy? It has not been lost, but instead has been changed into heat energy. The rubber of the bungee is warmer after the jump compared to before. The energy becomes heat, which first heats the rubber and then is carried away by the air as it cools the rubber.

The bungee jump illustrates one of the most important principles of science — energy can neither be created nor destroyed, but it can be changed in form. Potential gravitational energy changes into kinetic energy, kinetic energy changes into the potential energy of the stretched bungee, and then, finally, into heat energy.

The observation that energy can neither be created nor destroyed but can change form is known as the law of conservation of energy.

An airplane has three types of energy. One is potential energy due to its height above the earth. Another is kinetic energy due to its motion through the air. A third type is chemical energy in the fuel that it carries. The pilot of the airplane can trade altitude for speed — by lowering the nose of the aircraft, the

aircraft descends. It goes faster and gains kinetic energy. Or the pilot can raise the nose of the aircraft, in which case it will gain altitude but slowly lose speed. The pilot can push in the throttle and feed more fuel to the engine. Burning more fuel can make the plane gain altitude (potential energy) or gain speed (kinetic energy.)

Notice that total energy remains the same, but that individual types of energy can change. When two objects collide, such as the head of the hammer against the head of the nail, both lose their motion after the impact. Kinetic energy is lost. However, both gain heat energy.

Almost every time that energy changes form, the amount of heat energy increases. A car stops and its brakes become warmer. A battery changes chemical energy into electrical energy, and the battery becomes warm. The electric energy causes the filament of a light bulb to glow, and the bulb becomes warm. Heat energy increases at the expense of other energy sources.

SOLUTIONS

1. Battery and water behind the dam both have potential energy.

2. Both measure power.

3. Kinetic energy is the energy of motion.

Energy can neither be created nor destroyed.

T F   1.   Energy is a term that has been in use for more than 2,000 years.

A B   2.   Heat and light are examples of (A. matter   B. energy).

T F   3.   Energy can be changed from one form to another.

A B C D   4.   The equation $E = f \times d$ is used to find (A. efficiency
             B. mechanical advantage   C. momentum   D. work).

          5.   Work transfers _____ from one place to another.

A B C D   6.   Foot-pounds (English system) and joules (metric system) both
             measure (A. force   B. mass   C. power   D. work).

          7.   James Prescott Joule found how mechanical energy due to motion
             compares to _____ energy.

T F   8.   Pushing against a desk that does not move is an example of work.

A B   9.   The quantity that measures how quickly energy is supplied is called
             (A. work   B. power).

A B C   10.   The English and metric system units for measuring power are
             (A. calorie and joule   B. pound and newton   C. horsepower
             and watt).

A B   11.   The energy of motion is (A. kinetic   B. potential) energy.

T F   12.   Doubling mass of a moving object doubles its kinetic energy.

T F   13.   Doubling velocity of a moving object doubles its kinetic energy.

A B   14.   An object would gain more kinetic energy by (A. doubling its mass
             B. doubling its velocity).

A B   15.   Stored energy is called (A. kinetic   B. potential) energy.

A B C   16.   Almost every time that energy changes form, the amount of (A. heat
             B. kinetic   C. potential) energy increases.

6

Heat

One of the most difficult problems scientists faced was discovering the nature of heat. Although they did not know the exact nature of heat, they did realize that heat is a type of energy. They learned that the amount of heat in a substance depended upon three factors: temperature, amount of substance, and type of substance.

Suppose two identical objects have different temperatures. The hotter one — the one with the higher temperature — contains the greater amount of heat energy.

The amount of matter is the second factor. A cup of warm water may be at the same temperature as water in a swimming pool. But because of its greater size, the swimming pool contains more heat energy. You could melt a block of ice faster by dropping it into a swimming pool than by pouring the cup of water over it.

The third factor that determines the amount of heat in an

PROBLEMS

1. What is heat?

2. What stores heat better than most other everyday substances?

3. Why do islands in the ocean usually have a pleasant sea breeze?

Can You Propose Solutions?

object is the type of material. Substances do vary considerably in their heat capacity. One way to show heat capacity is to heat identical masses of different substances to the same temperature and then put them on a block of ice. The distance they melt into the ice is a measure of their heat capacity. Blocks of aluminum, iron, copper, zinc, and lead do not melt the same distance. Aluminum melts to a greater depth than the others. It has greater heat capacity than the other metals. Lead melts the least. It has the least heat capacity compared to the other metals.

Water stores heat especially well. For instance, water at room temperature has 30

energy changes the temperature of a kilogram iron bar by nine degrees, from 20°C to 29°C.

Weight for weight, water stores heat better than most other substances. Changing the temperature of water requires more heat energy than to change an identical mass of any other substance by the same temperature. Going the other way, as water cools, it releases more heat energy than the same mass of any other substance that cools by the same number of degrees.

The amount of heat in a body depends upon mass, temperature, and heat capacity of the substance. Scientists discovered this even before they knew what caused heat. Often, sci-

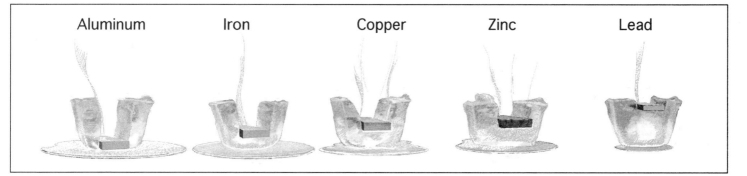

| Aluminum | Iron | Copper | Zinc | Lead |

You can measure heat capacity by heating identical masses of different substances and then placing them on a block of ice. Observe the different distances they melt into the ice.

times as much heat energy as an equal weight of lead at the same temperature.

Scientists call the heat capacity of a substance its specific heat. The specific heat is defined as the number of calories needed to raise one gram of the substance by a temperature of one degree Celsius. Water has a specific heat of 1.00. One calorie of heat energy will raise the temperature of one gram of water by one degree Celsius.

Water has a higher specific heat than almost any other everyday substance. Even metals do not hold heat as well as water. For instance, iron has a specific heat of 0.11, or $1/9$ the specific heat of water. Suppose a kilogram (1,000 grams) of water and a kilogram of iron were at room temperature, 20°C . Heating a kilogram of water from 20°C to 21°C takes 1,000 calories of heat energy. The same heat

entists must learn a great deal about a subject before they understand its true nature. For instance, they were able to build accurate thermometers despite not knowing exactly what property of a substance caused a rise or decline in temperature.

Heat and temperature are related, but they are not the same. The glowing filament of a flashlight bulb has a much higher temperature, about 5,400°F (2,982°C), than a burning piece of wood, about 600°F (282°C). You would expect, however, logs burning in a campfire to keep you warm better than a flashlight.

Temperature is measured with a thermometer. Nearly all materials expand when heated and shrink when cooled. Some thermometers use alcohol to measure temperature. A bulb at the bottom of the thermometer has a reservoir of alcohol. When temperature increases,

A pyrometer

the alcohol expands and rises up a thin tube inside the glass column.

One problem with an alcohol column is that alcohol is clear and difficult to see. Red or blue dye is usually added to make the alcohol column visible. Another problem with an alcohol thermometer is that alcohol is volatile. It evaporates readily. During hot weather, bubbles of alcohol vapor form in the thermometer. When the alcohol cools, the column of alcohol separates. The thermometer is ruined.

Unlike alcohol, mercury does not separate easily. The metal mercury is a liquid at room temperature. Although more expensive than alcohol, most precision thermometers use mercury. Mercury is opaque, so the position of the column is easier to read. Mercury expands at a constant rate, whether hot or cold. A one-degree change in temperature at the cold end of a mercury thermometer gives the same expansion as a one degree change in temperature at the warm end of the thermometer.

Mercury remains a liquid from -40°F (oddly enough, that is also equal to -40°C), to about 670°F (354°C.) Most kitchen ovens can reach a temperature of about 500°F (260°C).

How do you measure temperatures above the boiling temperature of mercury? For higher temperatures, other methods of measuring temperature must be used. Wire made of copper or other metals such as platinum conduct electricity better when hot than when cold. Electricity flows better as the temperature rises. A thermistor measures the flow of electricity through a wire to give the temperature. A thermistor that uses a platinum wire can measure temperatures up to 1,700°F (930°C).

Any substance begins glowing when heated to a temperature of about 1,000°F (538°C). The light that it emits changes color as the temperature increases. The color is the same regardless of the substance. Whether it is glass, metal, or pottery, the color it glows depends only on the temperature.

People who put the glaze on pottery used color to estimate the temperature inside their furnaces. Josiah Wedgwood, an English potter who lived in the 1700s, made some of the finest porcelain. He used color as a guide to the temperature: a dark red glow showed the temperature was 1,000°F (538°C), cherry red gave a temperature of 1,375°F (746°C), an object glowing orange was at 1,650°F (about 900°C), it became yellow at 1,800°F (982°C), and white hot at 2,200°F (about 1,200°C).

Today, a special device called a pyrometer (pyro means fire) has a filament similar to a light bulb. A dimmer switch adjusts the electricity flowing through the filament. When it glows the same color as the object being measured, the position of the dimmer switch shows the temperature. Temperatures as high as 2,400°F (1,315°C) can be measured in this way.

Daniel Fahrenheit (1686–1736), a German-born Dutch instrument maker, invented the first accurate mercury thermometer. His mercury thermometer helped him reveal an interesting property of water. He measured the temperature at which water boils to be 212°F (100°C). When water came to a boil, the temperature stayed at 212°F until all of the water boiled away. Adding more heat caused the water to boil faster, but the water did not get any hotter.

In the same way, he chilled water until it began to freeze. The water reached a temperature of 32°F (0°C), and then did not get any colder until all of the water had frozen.

Pure water has a fixed boiling and freezing temperature. Adding other substances can lower the freezing point. For instance, salt lowers the freezing point so that water melts at a lower temperature. Antifreeze (ethylene glycol) added to water can lower the freezing

For More Study—
Fahrenheit and Celsius Temperature Scales

Daniel Fahrenheit

Anders Celsius

Daniel Fahrenheit's thermometer has the freezing temperature of water at 32°F and the boiling temperature at 212°F. The number of degrees between the two temperatures is 180 Fahrenheit degrees: 212°F – 32°F = 180°F.

A Celsius degree is 1.8 times as large as a Fahrenheit degree: 180°F/100°C = 1.8°C/°F. But converting between Celsius and Fahrenheit temperatures is complicated by the fact that Celsius begins at 0°C for the melting temperature of water, but Fahrenheit has that same temperature equal to 32°F. Two conversion factors are involved: 1.8 and 32. To convert Fahrenheit to Celsius, you must first subtract 32°F to get them both to the same starting point and then divide by 1.8°F/°C. The equation is: °C = (°F – 32) / 1.8

As an example, convert 212°F to Celsius. First, subtract 32 and then divide by 1.8: 212°F – 32°F = 180°F   subtract 32°F

180°F/(1.8°F/°C) = 100°C   divide by 1.8°F

Daniel Fahrenheit discovered the freezing and boiling of water have fixed temperatures. Anders Celsius later developed a temperature scale that begins at 0° for freezing and 100° for the boiling temperature of water.

point so that water in a car's radiator does not freeze, even in the coldest winter.

Boiling is one way to cook some foods. Once boiling starts, the stove can be turned down because more heat merely boils the water faster but does not give a higher temperature.

How can foods be cooked at a higher temperature? One way is with a substance that has a higher boiling temperature. Cooking oil will boil at a higher temperature than water. For that reason, foods such as French fries cook faster in boiling oil than in boiling water

Normally, water boils at 212°F, but changes in air pressure also changes boiling temperature. A high air pressure gives a higher boiling temperature. Pressure cookers are closed containers. As pressure builds up in the container, water boils at a hotter temperature. A relief valve on the cooker prevents too much pressure.

A lower air pressure gives a lower boiling temperature for water. The summit of Mount Everest (28,028 feet) is far above more than

half of the atmosphere. Air pressure is reduced so that the boiling point of water is only 160°F (71°C). Some cities at higher elevation have to take into account the reduced air pressure. For instance, Denver, Colorado, is one mile above sea level. The boiling temperature of water is 203°F (95°C). At sea level, an egg can be hard boiled in three minutes. In Denver, it must be boiled for another minute.

About 40 years after Fahrenheit introduced his thermometer and temperature scale, Anders Celsius, a Swedish astronomer developed a new scale. He set the freezing temperature of water at 0°C and the boiling temperature of water at 100°C. The number of degrees between the two temperatures is 100 degrees Celsius: 100°C – 0°C = 100°C.

Most scientists use the Celsius temperature scale all the time, and they seldom have any reason to convert from one scale to the other. Sometimes they use a rule of thumb that gets what they call a "rough and ready" answer. For instance, for most temperatures in the range

John Dalton

10°C (a cool morning) to 35°C (a hot day), merely double the Celsius temperature and add 30. The temperature 10°C becomes 50°F: $(10 \times 2) + 30 = 20 + 30 = 50°F$, which is exactly the same as using the formulas. A temperature of 35°C becomes 100: $(35 \times 2) + 30 = 70 + 30 = 100$. In actual fact, 35°C is 95°F, so the rough and ready answer is off by 5 degrees, but you still get the idea that 35°C would be the temperature on a hot day.

Memorizing a few standard temperatures is also useful.

32°F = 0°C   (freezing temperature of water)
68°F = 20°C   (room temperature)
98.6°F = 37°C   (normal body temperature)
212°F = 100°C   (boiling temperature of water)

What is heat? For a long time, people thought of heat as a fluid. Water flows from a high point to a lower point. In the same way, scientists believed heat flowed from a place of high temperature to a place of a lower temperature. In the 1770s, the French chemist

Antoine Lavoisier listed heat as a substance. He called it caloric. According to Lavoisier, when a body became hot it did so because it gained caloric. When a body cooled, it did so because caloric flowed out of it.

Scientists tested this theory by weighing a metal rod while cool. Then they heated it red hot and weighed it again. The rod weighed the same. For caloric to be a substance, it must be weightless or nearly so.

Additional evidence against the idea of caloric came from Count Rumford. He'd been born in America. When the Revolutionary War started, he sided with the British.

The British put him to work building cannons in Bavaria. The factory drilled barrels from blocks of brass. The friction of the boring caused the metal to become intensely hot. Workers had to continually pour water over the machinery to cool it. Here was an endless supply of caloric that came from the friction of the drill. But Lavoisier had agreed that matter could neither be created nor destroyed. Caloric could not be a substance.

Count Rumford concluded that heat was a form of energy created by mechanical motion; that is, *kinetic energy*. If heat is a form of kinetic energy, then what moves? As the energy of the rotating drill went into the brass block, what in the block moved?

A few years later, an English schoolteacher named John Dalton advanced the atomic theory of matter. Dalton had begun by studying gases. He found that he could best explain his observations by thinking of gases as made of tiny particles that he called atoms. Later, he extended his ideas to include liquids and solids, too. The atomic theory of matter states that all matter is made of atoms. These atoms combine chemically to form molecules.

Dalton thought that gases were made of atoms which were far apart and could move independently. He drew their atoms like these circles.

What did the atomic theory of matter have to do with the kinetic theory of heat?

Robert Brown found the connection in 1827. Robert Brown, a Scottish botanist, was the son of a minister. He mixed pollen grains with water and observed the tiny pollen grains under a powerful microscope. By shining a strong beam of light into the drop of water from the side, the pollen grains appeared as bright specks of light. As he watched, the specks bounced around and made sudden, unexpected changes in direction. He repeated the experiment using very fine smoke particles. They zigzagged about, too. What caused the unexpected motion? He couldn't explain it, but he did report what he saw. The observation became know as Brownian motion.

Brownian motion is direct evidence that water molecules are in constant motion. Water molecules strike a pollen grain on all sides. If the particle is small enough, the collisions on one side are fewer than the collisions on the other side. The small particle is shoved about. The ceaseless, random motion of the water molecules shoved the pollen grains around.

Combining the atomic theory of matter with the kinetic theory of heat made it clear that heat is motion — the motion of atoms and molecules. In a solid, molecules are fixed in place. Heat causes them to vibrate back and forth. If the heat becomes too great, the molecules separate and the solid melts. In a liquid, the molecules can move about more freely than in a solid. Molecules in gases have the greatest freedom of all. They can charge about as independent bodies. Their motion changes only when they strike the walls of the container or each other.

Heat as a form of kinetic energy explains why the head of a nail gets hot when a hammer hits it. The kinetic energy of the hammer is transferred to the nail. The nail moves only a small amount. But the molecules inside the head of the nail vibrate about with a great speed. The visible motion of the hammer changes into the unseen motion of the molecules of the metal that make the nail. The molecules in the hammer also move so that it becomes warmer, too.

The heat content of a substance is the total kinetic energy of the molecules that make up the substance. You can increase the heat content by making the molecules move faster (higher temperature), or increase the number of molecules (more mass), or by switching the type of molecules (different substance).

Water molecules are in constant motion as seen when they cause a zigzag motion of pollen grains.

Temperature is the average kinetic energy of the molecules of an object. Heat and temperature are different. For instance, in the upper atmosphere of the earth, the energy of sunlight can cause molecules to zoom around at a speed that gives them a high temperature, but the air is so thin that the total amount of heat is very slight.

The formula for kinetic energy, $K.E. = \frac{1}{2}mv^2$, can be applied to a molecule. The mass of a single molecule is very small. However, a single small sample of gas contains billions of molecules. Their combined kinetic energy is what produces heat in a substance.

Heat is energy on the move. The direction of motion of heat is always from a warmer region to a cooler region. The hotter region gets cooler and the cooler region gets warmer. In other words, heat moves from a higher temperature (higher average kinetic energy) to a lower temperature (lower average kinetic energy). The average kinetic energy of the molecules becomes more nearly the same.

Conduction is one common way for heat to move. Conduction requires direct physical contact between the objects exchanging heat. Any substance, whether a solid, liquid, or gas will transfer heat by contact, but conduction is the only way that a solid can transfer heat.

Atoms in a solid are more or less fixed in place. Although the atoms do not move far from their average position, they do disturb their neighbors. Kinetic energy transfers from one atom to the nearby neighbor.

For instance, a metal poker is used to move wood around in a fireplace. If it is left in the fire, the heat will enter one end of the poker and eventually move to the other end. The atoms at the tip of the metal in the fire cannot move far from their fixed location. But they can move enough to upset those atoms near them. They begin moving, too. Eventually the disturbance moves the entire length of the rod.

Metals are good conductors of heat. Examples of metals include copper, aluminum, and iron. The atoms in most solids are locked in position and have limited movement. Scientists were puzzled as to how metals could conduct heat so well, but other substances with the same limited movement did not do as well. Why the difference between metals and nonmetals?

Metals conduct heat better than other materials because atoms of metals have electrons that are free to move about. Electrons move more freely and more readily transfer heat energy. Metals are good conductors of both heat and electricity because their electrons are free to roam from atom to atom.

Maybe you have noticed that the metal seat of a folding chair feels colder than one with a wooden seat, but if both chairs have been in the same environment, the metal seat is not colder. It only feels colder because the metal conducts heat away from your body better than the wooden seat. An object such as a metal seat feels colder because heat is going from your body into the object.

Nonmetals are poor conductors of heat. Examples of nonmetals include wood, fabric, building stone, and plastic. A person uses a special glove to pick up a hot poker because the heat does not readily travel through the fabric of the glove.

Choosing the correct material helps control the flow of heat. For instance, copper is a good conductor of heat. Although copper is expensive, some pots and pans have copper bottoms. The metal conducts heat from the burner or heating coil on a stove to the food being cooked in the pan.

Pizza is delivered in a padded holder that conducts heat poorly. The pizza arrives warm because the heat does not escape through the padded material. A hot pan is put on a potholder to keep it from scorching the table. The potholder is made of a fabric that conducts heat poorly.

Closely packed atoms conduct heat better than those in which the atoms are farther apart. Solids are usually better conductors than liquids, while liquids serve as better conductors than gases. Conduction is lowest in a gas because the molecules are so far apart. The fabric potholder is made of fibers that have a lot of air pockets. Heat moves slowly through the air pockets.

Fur and feathers are filled with air pockets. Animals such as the bear or duck can withstand cold temperatures. Their natural covering provides an insulating layer that prevents the loss of body heat. Snow also is filled with air pockets so it, too, acts as an insulator. Alaskan sled dogs can survive a blizzard by allowing snow to cover them. The snow does not supply heat. Instead, it prevents their own body heat from escaping and prevents the loss of heat directly to the cold winds of the blizzard.

Homes are insulated with fiberglass or blown-in insulation. They are poor conductors and also contain numerous air pockets. These materials conduct heat several thousand times more poorly than a metal. In the time it takes heat to travel through a few inches of the insulation, it would travel through several thousand feet of copper wire.

Convection is another common way for the transfer of heat. Convection is heat transfer in a liquid or gas by the circulation of currents. Most substances expand as they are heated. The molecules gain energy and move about more vigorously. They collide with one another and push one another apart. The substance becomes less dense. The cooler and denser surrounding fluid constantly puts pressure on the lighter region and causes it to rise. As the less dense fluid rises, the more dense fluid moves in and takes its place. The motion sets up currents that circulate heat.

The water at the bottom of a teakettle is heated by conduction. The water becomes less dense and rises. This sets up a current that draws in more cold water. The process circulates energy so the water in the kettle becomes uniformly hot, although only the bottom of the kettle contacts the source of the heat.

A candle burns because the heat of the flame heats the air. The rising warm air draws in cooler air with a fresh supply of oxygen. The flame of a candle flickers because of the rising air current.

Convection currents only occur when gravity is present. In the weightlessness of space, air would not rise around a candle flame. The oxygen near the flame would become exhausted. In a few minutes, the candle would go out.

Islands in the tropics are noted for their sea breezes. During the day, the land becomes hotter than the water, so air flows in from the ocean to the land to replace the rising air. A sea breeze is a convection current.

Radiation is the third way that heat can move from one place to another. In this process, heat energy is transferred by elec-

James Watt, inventor of the steam engine, as a child.

tromagnetic radiation. Light is a form of electromagnetic energy, as are infrared rays. Infrared rays are sometimes called heating rays. The heating coil of a toaster gets hot enough to glow with visible light, but invisible infrared rays produce most of the heat.

Radiant heat is the only method of heat transfer that can pass through the vacuum of space. Transfer of heat by radiation travels at the speed of light. It can go great distances with practically no energy loss, especially in a vacuum. Heat from the sun arrives at the earth in the form of radiant energy.

A microwave oven is an example of a heat source that uses radiant energy. When you warm up a leftover slice of pizza in a microwave, the heating is done by radiant energy. The microwave generates electromagnetic waves that strike the food and heats it.

Inventors have looked for ways to use heat to do work. A heat engine takes heat energy and changes it into mechanical energy. The mechanical energy can then be used to do work. Sometimes the mechanical energy is used to generate electricity. Often, however, the heat engine does work directly. Old fashioned steam locomotives, gasoline engines used in everyday means of transportation such as cars and motorcycles, and jet aircraft, all use heat engines.

The first successful heat engine was the steam engine. Scottish inventor James Watt developed the steam engine in the late 1700s. His invention made the industrial revolution possible. Like all heat engines, a steam engine works because heat flows from a hot region to a cooler region. The hot region is called the heat source. The cooler region is called the heat sink.

For any heat engine to work, the heat source and heat sink must be different in temperature. Heat, like water, must flow to produce energy. For instance, a hydroelectric plant generates electricity as water falls from a high level above the dam to a lower level at the

Islands in the tropics are noted for their sea breezes.

foot of the dam. The greater the height from which it falls, the greater the energy it can produce. In the same way, heat must travel from a higher temperature to a lower temperature to generate energy. The difference in temperature, not the actual temperature, is what matters. The greater the difference in temperature, the more work the heat engine can do. No matter how hot the heat source, if the heat sink is the same temperature, then the engine can do no work.

In both automobile and high-speed jet aircraft engines, the combustion chambers are hotter than the atmosphere. The greater the difference in temperature, the better the engine performs. It converts a higher percentage of the fuel into motion. A difference in temperature is essential, and the greater the difference, the better.

For years, inventors have been trying to take advantage of the difference in water temperature in the oceans. The average surface temperature of ocean water is about 65°F (18°C). Near the bottom of a deep ocean, the temperature stays at a uniform temperature of 34°F (1°C) year around. A heat engine could use the difference in temperature to generate electricity. However, because the difference in temperature is so slight, no method has yet been developed to extract useful work.

If you left a cup of hot chocolate sitting on a table, you expect that after a while it would get cold. You expect the heat to go from the hot chocolate into the cooler surroundings. In a chilly room, the heat rising above the cup would show that the liquid is steaming hot. The heat travels from the hot liquid into the air by convection and into the cup and table under it by conduction.

Sometimes we describe the direction of the motion in terms of things getting colder. If we drop some ice cubes into warm lemonade, we may say that the ice cubes make the liquid colder. Actually, the reverse is what is happening. Rather than cold going from the ice cubes into the liquid, heat is traveling from the liquid into the ice cubes. Over time, heat causes ice cubes to melt.

We would be astonished if heat traveled from cold to hot. If you placed logs in a cold and empty fireplace, you would not expect heat to flow into the logs and become so concentrated that the logs ignite on their own. Heat naturally travels from hot to cold, but never the other way.

Thermodynamics is the study of the movement of heat. The word thermodynamics is from two Greek words, *thermo* meaning heat and *dynamics* meaning power.

For More Study: Efficiency of Heat Engines

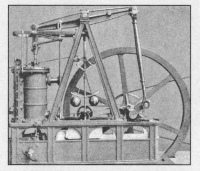

In the early 1800s, French physicist Nicolas Carnot investigated James Watt's steam engine. The engine was not very efficient. Only about 7 percent of the heat energy of burning fuel actually ended up producing mechanical motion. More than 93 percent of the heat energy was wasted. Why?

James Watt invented the first successful steam engine.

Some people believed that by building the steam engine more carefully, removing friction, and reducing heat loss by insulating the combustion chambers, efficiency could be greatly improved. However, Carnot found a surprising result. After friction and unintended heat loss are eliminated, the only way to improve the efficiency is to increase the difference in temperature between heat source and heat sink. His discovery applied to all heat engines and not to steam engines alone.

The maximum efficiency of a heat engine depends upon the maximum and minimum temperatures. For a steam engine, maximum temperature is the temperature of steam inside the cylinder. Its minimum temperature is the temperature of the steam after it condenses into water. For an automobile engine, the maximum temperature is the temperature of the gas and air mixture right after combustion. The minimum temperature is the temperature of the exhaust.

Carnot's equation gives the maximum efficiency as the difference in the heat source and heat sink temperature divided by the heat source temperature. As an equation: Efficiency = $(T_1 - T_2)/T_1$ with T_1 the heat source temperature and T_2 the heat sink temperature.

The temperatures are measured in degrees Kelvin. The Kelvin temperature scale begins at absolute zero, the coldest temperature possible, and uses the same size degrees as the Celsius thermometer. A Celsius temperature is changed to Kelvin temperature by adding 273 degrees. For example, 0°C is 273 K and 100°C is 373 K. (The Kelvin temperature scale does not use the little degree symbol, °, in front of the K.)

Suppose steam in an engine is heated to 200°C (heat source, or T_1) before condensing to 50°C as water (heat sink, or T_2). To find the maximum efficiency, first change the temperatures to degrees Kelvin by adding 273: $T_1 = 200°C = 473$ K and $T_2 = 50°C = 323$ K. Next, subtract heat sink temperature from heat source temperature and divide by the heat sink temperature.

$$
\begin{aligned}
\text{Efficiency} &= (T_1 - T_2)/T_1 \\
&= (473 \text{ K} - 332 \text{ K})/473 \text{ K} \\
&= (241 \text{ K})/(473 \text{ K}) \\
&= 0.298
\end{aligned}
$$

The efficiency of 0.298 or about 30 percent is the absolute maximum efficiency that a heat machine operating at those temperatures can produce. A perfectly made machine would output only 30 calories of energy for every 100 calories of heat input. No steam engine, gasoline engine, or jet engine can be made mechanically perfect. They do have friction and are not perfectly insulated against unintended heat loss. Actual efficiency will be less than the theoretical efficiency.

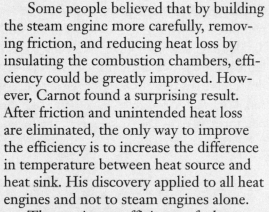

The first law of thermodynamics is the law of conservation of energy.

The second law of thermodynamics states that heat naturally flows from a region of high temperature to a region of lower temperature but never the reverse.

All forms of energy — chemical, electrical, nuclear, light, and all the other forms — power machines that do work. But these energy sources change into the random motion of atoms and molecules that make heat energy. Friction converts mechanical energy into heat. Resistance in electrical lines changes electrical energy into heat. Matter absorbs radiant energy and changes into heat. As forms of energy do work, some heat is generated.

No machine can fully take advantage of the energy that heat contains. The energy does not disappear, but it cannot be fully used. The spreading of heat at the expense of other energy sources is another consequence of the second law of thermodynamics.

As heat spreads, it increases the amount of random motion of molecules. For example, snowflakes are noted for their pattern and design. When the snow melts and becomes water, the orderly pattern is lost. Motion of molecules in liquid water is disorganized. The molecules bounce aimlessly in all directions. Brownian motion in which tiny pollen grains are shoved in a zigzag course by water molecules reveals this random motion. Water molecules in steam are even more disorganized.

Entropy is the term used to measure disorganization. Physicists believe that the entropy of the universe — its disorganization — is always increasing. The second law of thermodynamics is also known as the law of entropy.

Is it possible to reverse the flow of heat? Can it be made to go from a cooler region to a warmer region? Yes, but to make that happen, work is required. Air conditioners and refrigerators are known as heat pumps. They reverse the natural flow of heat. To do so requires work. An air conditioner uses the energy of electricity to operate a motor that moves heat from inside the home to the outside.

Could a heat pump remove all of the heat from a closed container? As heat is removed, the atoms would move more and more slowly. Finally, almost all motion would cease. The atoms would have zero heat energy and zero entropy. Such a condition is known as absolute zero. Scientists have calculated that -459.67°F (-273.15°C) is the coldest temperature possible. However, the colder an object gets, the more vigorously heat flows into it. It is impossible to remove all the heat from an object.

The third law of thermodynamics states that absolute zero can never be obtained. At one time, scientists believed all motion would cease at absolute zero. Now they think that some motion remains, but it is unavailable to do work.

Scientists use liquid helium and special magnetic alloys to extract heat so that the temperature gets within one hundred thousandths (0.00001 K) of absolute zero. Getting to that low temperature is especially difficult, and measuring the temperature near absolute zero requires skill, too. One way to measure extremely cold temperatures is to measure changes in the magnetic property of certain alloys.

SOLUTIONS

1. Heat is the energy of motion of atoms and molecules.

2. Water has a high specific heat.

3. Convection of air from ocean to shore gives a sea breeze.

   Heat is usually produced as energy changes form.

A B C D   1.   Heat is a type of (A. energy   B. force   C. matter   D. temperature).

            2.   The three factors that determine the heat contained in an object are type of substance, mass, and _____.

A B   3.   The one that stores heat better is (A. iron   B. water).

A B   4.   A thermometer works on the principle that most substances (A. contract B. expand) when heated.

A B C D   5.   The two most common substances used in thermometers are colored alcohol and (A. cooking oil   B. ethylene glycol   C. mercury   D. molten salt).

T F   6.   Scientists are unable to measure temperatures greater than 1,700°F.

A B C D   7.   The scientist who discovered that pure water has a fixed boiling and freezing temperature was (A. Anders Celsius   B. Antoine Lavoisier C. Daniel Fahrenheit   D. John Dalton).

A B   8.   High air pressure causes water to boil at a (A. higher   B. lower) temperature.

T F   9.   Heat is the motion of atoms and molecules.

A B   10.   Heat is a form of (A. kinetic   B. potential) energy.

A B C   11.   Heat moving from one end of a metal fireplace poker to the other end is an example of heat transfer by (A. conduction   B. convection   C. radiation).

A B   12.   The one that conducts heat better is (A. copper   B. wood).

A B   13.   Fur, feathers, and other substances with air pockets conduct heat (A. poorly B. well).

A B C   14.   A sea breeze is set in motion because of (A. conduction   B. convection C. radiation).

T F   15.   Heat is transferred from the sun to earth by radiation.

T F   16.   A steam engine works because heat flows from a hot region to a cold region.

A B   17.   A heat engine works best when the temperature change from heat source to heat sink is (A. about the same   B. greatly different).

T F   18.   Moving heat energy in a direction opposite to its normal flow requires work.

For more study

     19.   The maximum efficiency possible for a machine that produces energy from the difference of ocean water at 18°C at the surface and 1°C at depth is _____.

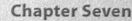
States of Matter

The three states of matter are solid, liquid, and gas.

To contrast solid, liquid, and gas, think of a column made of each one in an empty room. A solid column of the metal lead has a definite shape and volume. It will stand of its own accord in the room and not move. Now imagine what would happen if the column were made of water. The water would collapse to the floor, spread out to the walls, and flow into the lowest levels. It would have the same volume as before the collapse, but the shape would change. Finally, think about a column made of carbon dioxide gas. When released, the gas would diffuse throughout the room and fill every nook and cranny. The gas readily changes shape and volume. A gas released in a container will expand to fill the container.

We say that the metal lead is a solid, water is a liquid, and carbon dioxide is a gas. However,

PROBLEMS

1. How can cars ride more smoothly?

2. What gives the strong spray to water from a shower nozzle?

3. What causes a hot air balloon to rise?

Can You Propose Solutions?

those descriptions are not always true. Lead melts at 662°F (328°C), so lead is a liquid on the planet Mercury, which has a daytime temperature of about 810°F (about 430°C).

Any substance, whether solid, liquid, or gas can be changed into another state by being heated or cooled. For instance, lead becomes molten (liquid) at 662°F (328°C). It boils at 3,164°F (1,740°C) and changes to a gas.

Wood is highly elastic. It will spring back to its original shape, as seen when an archer pulls back on a wooden bow deforming it before releasing an arrow. Once the arrow is released, the wood comes back to its original form.

Oxygen is a gas at room temperature, but if cooled to -297°F (-183°C) it becomes a liquid, and at -361°F (218°C) it become a solid.

Usually, we think of a substance as a solid if it is a solid at room temperature, but scientists are more specific. They use standard temperature and pressure. Standard temperature is 32°F (0°C). Standard pressure is equal to the pressure that earth's atmosphere exerts at sea level. Scientists would say that lead is a solid at standard temperature and pressure.

Another property of solids — but not liquids or gases — is elasticity. Solids resist changes in their shape. In addition, many solids spring back to their original shape when compressed, twisted, or pulled. Physicists say that a substance is elastic if it returns to its original shape. A rubber band is elastic, not because it will stretch, but because it will snap back when released.

We do not usually think of steel, glass, or wood as elastic, but they are highly elastic because they will spring back to their original shape. For instance, the first bows for shooting arrows were made of wood. The motion given to the arrow came from the spring of the wooden bow after being deformed by the archer's pull on the string.

Glass marbles rebound when they strike one another. Each one keeps its original shape. They are elastic. Lead, on the other hand, is not as elastic. Two lead balls strike one another with a dull thud and are mis-shapen after the collision.

One quick way to measure the elasticity of an object is to see if they bounce and are not deformed by a collision. Suppose you dropped a glass marble, a lead ball, and a ball of dough to a hard, smooth concrete floor. The glass will bounce the highest (provided it doesn't shatter). It will bounce to about 90 percent of the height from which it was dropped. It is highly elastic. The lead does not bounce as high. It is less elastic. The ball of dough strikes the floor and stays there. It has zero elasticity.

Steel is also highly elastic. Steel springs are used in many devices because of this property.

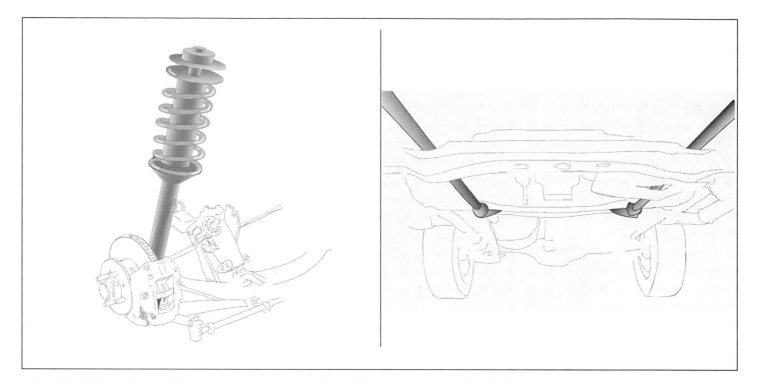

Steel is highly elastic. Above we see two examples of this elasticity, as shock absorbers to give cars smoother rides.

Retractable ballpoint pens use the elastic property of steel. When you click the pen, a coiled steel spring causes the pen to retract.

Many modern front-wheel-drive cars have McPherson struts as part of their suspension system. Inside the strut is a coiled steel spring wrapped around a shock absorber. Heavy trucks have torsion bars, which replace steel springs. They twist and untwist, thus cushioning the shocks of bumps that might damage a heavy truck.

Orthodontists correct poorly aligned teeth by twisting a wire and attaching it to the teeth. Over time, the continued elastic restoring force of the twisted wire straightens the teeth. All of these devices work because steel is highly elastic.

Robert Hooke made the first scientific examination of elasticity. He lived in the 1600s at about the same time as Isaac Newton. The Royal Society, a group of scientists in England, employed Robert Hooke to show two or three interesting experiments each week. As the years passed, Robert Hooke did thousands of experiments.

While studying elasticity, he developed what became known as Hooke's law: the amount a solid object bends is directly proportional to the force acting on it. Double the force and the object bends twice as much.

You can experiment with Hooke's law by firmly clamping one end of a yardstick to the end of a table. From the other end, hook a plastic bag and begin dropping in identical weights such as identical coins, bolts, or children's building blocks. With each weight, the yardstick will bend down toward the floor. Measure the amount it bends after each weight is put in the plastic bag. When the weight doubles, the yardstick bends twice as much. When the weight triples, the yardstick bends three times as much.

If you add too much weight, the yardstick may no longer follow Hooke's law. The stick has reached its elastic limit and is about to break. As a solid is deformed, forces pull to return the molecules to their normal positions. But if the molecules are pulled too far out of alignment, the forces acting among them are broken. The solid does not return to its original size and shape.

Solids, liquids, and gases all exert pressure. For solids, the pressure is due to the weight of the solid divided by the surface area in contact with the ground. As an equation: pressure = weight/area.

Spreading force over a greater area reduces pressure. Sometimes a child skating on thin ice will break through. When the emergency workers respond, they lay a ladder on the ice and then crawl along the ladder to tie a rope to the victim. The ice holds, although the rescuer weighs far more than the child. The ladder spreads the weight of the adult over a greater area.

Liquids press against the sides of the container. The pressure depends on the height of the water column. Imagine a bucket filled with water that springs three leaks along its side. One is near the top, one near the middle, and the third near the bottom. Water streams through all three holes. But water squirts farther from the bottom one because pressure is greater there.

Water towers not only store water, but also provide the pressure that sends the water through pipes to homes and businesses. Two tanks, one large and one small but at the same

Robert Hooke

Robert Hooke (English scientist, 1635–1703) was born on the Isle of Wight, a small island south of the United Kingdom in the English Channel. He was frail and undersized as a child. Throughout his life, he suffered severe headaches and often could not sleep except in short catnaps. He became an orphan at age 13. He worked his way through college by waiting tables.

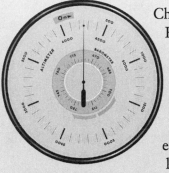

A barometer is a device to measure air pressure.

In 1663, the Royal Society of London employed Hooke to demonstrate interesting new ideas each week. He held this position for more than 40 years. He did other work as well. He helped Robert Boyle build and experiment with an air pump. Following the Great Fire of London in 1666, he served as Christopher Wren's main assistant in rebuilding the city.

Hooke designed an improved microscope. While studying a thin slice of cork, he saw a regular pattern of tiny, honeycomb-like pores. He called them cells. His finding was the first clue that cells are the building blocks of life.

After one of the meetings of the Royal Society, Robert Hooke, architect Christopher Wren, and astronomer Edmund Halley met and discussed the nature of gravity. Hooke stated that gravity grew weaker by the square of the distance. Isaac Newton succeeded in proving Hooke correct and acknowledged Hooke's contribution to the law of gravity.

Hooke invented or improved many scientific instruments, including the air pump, microscope, barometer, and the first small watch that kept accurate time. His best-known discovery was Hooke's law of elasticity: the amount a solid is deformed is directly proportional to the force acting on it. Spring scales for weighing produce in supermarkets use this principle.

Because of his frequent headaches, lack of sleep, and pressure of doing so many different tasks, Hooke was often grumpy. His friends overlooked this because they knew that pain racked his body. He also had the misfortune of living at the same time as Isaac Newton. Hooke's discoveries would have made him the greatest scientist of his time, but Isaac Newton was the greatest scientist of all time and overshadowed him.

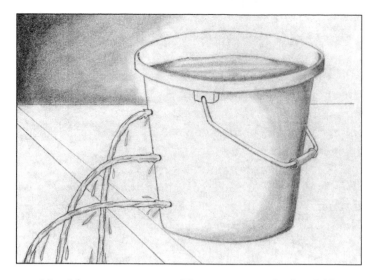

Liquids exert pressure. The pressure of a liquid is proportional to the product of both density and depth.

height, produce the same pressure. A large tank will supply more water than a small tank but the water pressure is equal. A garden hose will squirt water as far whether the source is a large tank or a small one. What matters is the height of the tank.

The pressure of a liquid is proportional to the product of both density and depth: pressure = density × depth. Gasoline has about ¾ the density of water. A column of gasoline exerts a pressure only about 75 percent as great as a column of water at the same height.

Blaise Pascal, a French scientist, discovered an important property of fluids in 1654. He found that pressure acts throughout a container. Suppose a closed container is filled with a liquid. If pressure is exerted anywhere on the liquid in a closed container, then it acts equally on the walls, top, and bottom of the container. The fact that pressure in a liquid acts equally in all directions is known as Pascal's principle.

Pascal's principle explains the workings of a hydraulic press. Today, hydraulic presses are used in hair salons to raise chairs, to activate the brakes of cars, and to raise loads with hydraulic jacks.

A hydraulic press has a tank that contains a fluid, usually thick oil, and two cylinders of different sizes. Pushing down on a piston in the smaller cylinder transmits pressure unchanged throughout the container and to the second piston. The pressure causes the larger piston to rise.

According to Pascal's principle, the pressure on the surface of the small piston and the pressure on the surface of the large piston are equal. The total force on the larger piston is greater because it has a greater surface area. A small force applied to the small piston produces a much greater force on the larger piston.

One simple type of hydraulic press is a jack that raises heavy trucks to change their tires. A person can pump a hydraulic jack handle with a few pounds of pressure to lift a truck that weighs several tons. At first this may seem to be something for nothing. Of course, there is a catch. The smaller piston must move through a greater distance than the larger piston.

For instance, a DC2 airplane was one of the first airplanes to carry passengers. When the plane was ready to land, the copilot lowered the wheels by hand by raising and lowering the handle to pump them down by hydraulic pressure. The co-pilot had to pump about 70 times on the handle to lower the wheels a few feet.

Air and other gases act like fluids. Pascal's principle applies equally well to gases and liquids. Like water, gases transmit pressure in all directions. The air inside a balloon pushes outward at right angles against the balloon.

Another property of solids, liquids, and gases is density. Density is a measure of the

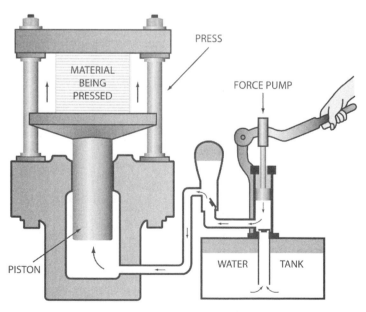

Diagram of an hydraulic press

mass of a substance compared to its volume. The equation is density = mass / volume. Density of solids and liquids is usually measured in pounds per cubic feet, lbs/ft^3, or grams per cubic centimeter, g/cm^3.

Because of the empty space between molecules, the density of a gas is always less than the density of the same substance as a liquid or solid. Usually, the density is around 1,000 times less. The density of water is 1.0 g/cm^3, but steam has a density of 0.00061 g/cm^3, which is 1,600 times less.

To avoid small numbers, scientists prefer to state the density of gases in ounces per cubic foot, or grams per liter. A liter is a little larger than a quart. Air has a density of about 0.0013 grams per cubic centimeter, which is equivalent to about 1.5 ounces per cubic foot, or 1.25 grams per liter.

Buoyancy is the upward force exerted against a solid placed in a fluid. If you take a heavy concrete block and lower it into water, the block will seem to become lighter. More than 2,000 years ago, Archimedes, the great

Blaise Pascal

Blaise Pascal (1623–1662, French scientist) came from a wealthy family, but he suffered the tragedy of his mother dying when he was but three years old. His father ensured that his son received a good education. Pascal's father hired tutors who educated him at home.

In 1630, Pascal and his father moved to Paris. There father and son attended scientific meetings. While still a teenager, Pascal wrote his first scientific report, one about conic sections. His father became a tax collector. Pascal reduced the drudgery of long arithmetic calculations by building a mechanical calculator, the first of its kind.

Pascal lived at about the same time as Galileo and Kepler. Like them, he understood the importance of experiments. At sea level, atmospheric pressure was 14.7 pounds per square inch. This is the weight of a one-inch square column of air that extends from the surface of the earth into space.

Air pressure gauge

Pascal believed that as one gained altitude, air pressure would decrease. To test this theory, he needed to take barometer readings from a high mountain. Pascal was not athletic, so he talked his brother-in-law into carrying a barometer up the side of Puy-de-Dôme Mountain. The barometer showed that air pressure did become less with height. A barometer could serve as an altimeter and measure the height above sea level.

Throughout his life, Pascal worked to better understand Christianity. From 1654 on, he spent most of his time in religious matters. He wrote books on religion that conveyed his passionate interest in living a Christian life. He died at age 39. During his short life, Pascal left his mark in a variety of fields including physics, mathematics, geometry, and Christian literature.

The metric unit for pressure, the pascal, is named in his honor. A pascal is equal to a pressure of one newton per square meter.

Greek scientist, experimented with buoyancy and arrived at what has become known as Archimedes' law of buoyancy. He found that the lifting force acting on a solid object immersed in water is equal to the weight of the water shoved aside by the object.

Water weighs about 64 pounds per cubic foot. A concrete block that is one foot on each side weighs about 204 pounds. When the concrete block is under water, it will weigh 140 pounds. It shoves aside 64 pounds of water and weighs 64 pounds less: 204 lbs – 64 lbs = 140 lbs.

Archimedes' law of buoyancy also applies equally well to gases and liquids. Not only does the law of buoyancy explain why a rock is lighter underwater, but it also explains how a hot air balloon rises into the air. Air in the balloon is heated to about 300°F (149°C). Hot air expands and weighs less for the same volume. Hot air weighs about 1.0 oz/ft^3, rather than 1.5 oz/ft^3. This gives the balloon 0.5 ounce of lift for every cubic foot inside the balloon.

For a passenger-carrying balloon to soar into the sky, the balloon must be big enough to lift the passengers and the weight of the balloon. Sport balloons range in size from 65,000 to 105,000 cubic feet in volume and stand about 70 feet tall. A 65,000 cubic feet balloon gives about 32,500 ounces of lift, or about 2,000 pounds.

Three properties of a gas — volume, temperature, and pressure — are related to each other. Whenever one changes, so do the other two.

Robert Boyle studied gases in the 1650s. He asked the question, "What happens to the space occupied by a gas when it is put under pressure?" Boyle proved that volume and pressure are related in a predictable way. Doubling the pressure squeezes a gas into one-half its original space. Three times as much pressure reduces the volume to one third. Boyle's law states that the volume of a gas is inversely proportional to the pressure. They are inversely related because as one goes up the other goes down.

It is interesting that Boyle's law applies equally well to any gas. Hydrogen, oxygen, and nitrogen all follow Boyle's law. So do mixtures of gases such as the atmosphere. Scientists are especially pleased when a large number of different observations can be summarized by a single natural law.

In 1787, Jacques Charles, a French chemist, discovered another gas law. He looked at how temperature and volume are related while he kept the pressure the same. Everyone knows that when a gas is heated it expands. When it cools it contracts. Jacques Charles found the exact factor by which a gas expands when heated. Heating a gas one degree Celsius increased its volume by $1/273$ of its volume at zero degrees Celsius. When he cooled the gas by one degree Celsius, the volume decreased by $1/273$ of its original volume. His law applied equally well to any gas.

Charles's discovery brought up an interesting question. What happens to a gas that is chilled to −273 degrees Celsius? According to Charles's law, its volume would shrink to zero. Could a gas disappear entirely? No, because before it reached −273 degrees Celsius, the gas would condense to a liquid. The gas laws do not apply to liquids.

Envelope

Gas Burner

Basket

A hot air balloon develops 0.5 ounce of lift for every cubic foot of hot air in the balloon.

Joseph Gay-Lussac, who lived at about the same time as Jacques Charles, expressed the relationship between temperature and pressure of a gas. For constant volume, the temperature of a gas is directly proportional to the pressure. As gas is forced into a container and the pressure goes up, the temperature increases. When the gas is released from the container, and the pressure decreases, so does the temperature.

The discoveries of Boyle, Charles, and Gay-Lussac can be combined into a single statement known as the ideal gas law: pressure times volume of a gas divided by the temperature is a constant. As an equation: $(P \times V)/T = k$, with P the pressure, V the volume, T the temperature and k a constant. A constant is a fixed number that does not change. If any two of the quantities change, the remaining one will automatically change too so that the constant remains the same.

The equation relating pressure, volume, and temperature is known as the ideal gas law. It applies equally well to any gas with only slight variation. The fact that there is some variation means that no one particular gas follows the equation exactly. Only an "ideal" gas does that, and no ideal gas exists.

Suppose oxygen is released at one end of a tube and hydrogen at the other end. They will expand until they fill the container. Two gases in a container mix together thoroughly. This process is called diffusion.

Robert Boyle (English Chemist, 1627–1691)

Robert Boyle was born in Ireland, although his family was English. He was the seventh son of the Great Earl of Cork, a man of immense wealth. To keep his son from becoming spoiled, the Great Earl arranged for Robert to live with a poor Irish family. Once his formal schooling began, he lived in his father's castle where he was educated by tutors.

Robert Boyle

When he became an adult, Robert believed the future of science lay with the experimental method. His motto, "nothing by mere authority" rejected the idea that ancient books had all of the answers. He and a group of experimental scientists held informal talks in each other's homes. Boyle called the group "the invisible college."

In 1654, Boyle moved to Oxford, not to attend college, but to be closer to scientists who agreed as he did in the importance of experiments to verify scientific discoveries. With the assistance of Robert Hooke, he built an improved air pump. They proved that sound does not carry in a vacuum. They confirmed Galileo's belief that a feather and a lump of lead would fall at the same speed in a vacuum. Robert Boyle published *Touching the Spring of the Air* in 1660. The book contained Boyle's law that the volume of a gas varies inversely to the pressure.

Boyle urged his fellow scientists to report their experiments quickly so others might know of new discoveries. In 1663, he led in the successful effort to charter the Royal Society as a formal scientific body patterned after the invisible college.

Besides his scientific investigations, Robert Boyle learned Hebrew and Greek to pursue his study of Scripture. When he died in London, his will left his scientific collection and equipment to the Royal Society and provided for a yearly lecture for "proving the Christian religion against the attack of infidels."

Pass by a cinnamon roll shop at a mall and the freshly made rolls can be smelled from a great distance. The vapors rise in the air and travel well away from their origin. The vapors mix with the air by diffusion.

Diffusion is the mixing of two substances by the ceaseless motion of their molecules. Liquids will mix, too, but it takes longer. For instance, the muddy waters of the Missouri River flow into the blue water of the Upper Mississippi at St. Louis, Missouri. For several miles downstream, the two flows can be detected before they thoroughly mix. Solids mix hardly at all, but it does occur. When two pieces of metal are put in tight contact with one another, over several hundred years molecules will transfer between the two.

Of the three states of matter, gases diffuse most quickly. Their molecules move around more freely than the molecules of liquids or solids.

Thomas Graham of Glasgow, Scotland, made another important discovery about gases. He proved that different gases diffuse at different speeds. The rate of diffusion of a gas is inversely proportional to the square root of its molecular weight.

For instance, oxygen gas is 16 times as heavy as the same volume of hydrogen gas. Hydrogen gas diffuses four times as fast as oxygen. The number 4 is the square root of 16.

James Clerk Maxwell challenged himself to develop a single theory about gases that combined all of the work of the other scientists. He began with simple assumptions and calculated how gases would act using those assumptions alone. Then he compared his predictions with the known properties of gases.

He assumed that molecules travel in straight lines except when they collide with one another or with the walls of their container. During collisions, some molecules gain velocity and others lose velocity. Overall, however, Maxwell assumed the average speed of all the molecules was constant. The container of gas as a whole did not lose kinetic energy, the energy of motion.

From these simple assumptions, he developed what became known as the kinetic theory of gases. The kinetic theory of gases explained the relationships among temperature, volume, and pressure of a gas.

According to Boyle's law, if the volume of a gas is cut in half, the pressure doubles. The kinetic theory of gases easily explained this. Compressing the gas into a smaller volume reduced the average distance a molecule traveled before it hit the walls of the container. If it had to travel only half as far, it collided twice as often, and produced twice the pressure.

Maxwell's Assumptions about Gases

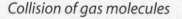

Collision of gas molecules

1. Gas molecules are small compared with the average distance between them.
2. Because of the distances separating them, gas molecules exert practically no forces upon one another except when they collide.
3. Gas molecules move rapidly and freely in all directions.
4. Gas molecules frequently collide with one another and with the walls of their container. However, the collisions are completely elastic. No energy is lost.

Daniel Bernoulli (Swiss Physicist, 1700–1782)

Daniel Bernoulli's father was a mathematician and earned a very limited salary at that profession. He insisted that his son, Daniel, become a doctor. Daniel Bernoulli became a physician, but his real passion was mathematics and physics. He never practiced medicine, although he studied the action of the lungs and described the physics behind their workings.

Russia invited Daniel to teach mathematics in that country in 1726. Newton's laws had been applied to large objects such as the moon, planets, and projectiles. While in Russia, Bernoulli applied Newton's laws of motion to smaller particles such as the molecules in gases and liquids. With only a few basic assumptions, he derived Boyle's law that the pressure of a gas is inversely related to its volume. About 100 years later, James Clerk Maxwell would expand on Bernoulli's preliminary work and establish the kinetic theory of gases.

After seven years in Russia, Bernoulli returned to Switzerland and became a

Bernoulli's principle applies to cleanly designed modern day cars.

professor of physics. He was one of the first scientists to fully apply the law of conservation of energy to gases.

He showed, for example, that the motion of a fluid gave it kinetic energy, and the pressure of the fluid gave it potential energy. A fluid that increased speed had to lose pressure to keep the total energy constant. This is known as Bernoulli's principle: as the speed of a moving fluid increases, the pressure within the fluid decreases.

Bernoulli realized that fluids such as air or water that flow in layers do so more smoothly and require less energy than fluids that are filled with eddies and swirls. As a practical application, he designed the hull of ships so that they cut through the water with a less turbulent flow. This increased the efficiency and speed of the ships. Today, high-speed vehicles including cars and airplanes take advantage of this fact. A vehicle is said to have a clean design if it can pass through the air without causing turbulence.

According to Charles's law, when a gas cools, the pressure becomes less. Once again, this can be explained in terms of molecules in motion. Temperature is a measure of the average speed of molecules. If they cool, they move more slowly and strike one another and their container less often. With fewer collisions, the pressure is less.

A gas such as air contains energy. Some of this energy is potential energy stored in the pressure of the air. Some of the energy is the kinetic energy of the air's motion. If the speed of the gas does not change, each of the two forms of energy remains constant. But one can be traded for the other.

When air is forced into a container, the air no longer is in motion, but the container

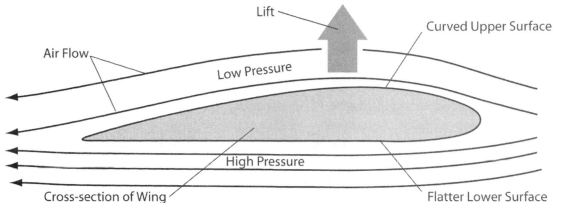

Lift
Air Flow
Low Pressure
Curved Upper Surface
Cross-section of Wing
High Pressure
Flatter Lower Surface

Differences in pressure over the wing give an airplane enough lift to support it.

of motion. Hurricanes and tornadoes reveal their approach by a sudden drop in air pressure.

An airplane wing gets its lift because air moving across the top of a wing goes faster than air under the wing. The greater speed comes at the expense of pressure, which is reduced. The difference in the pressure over the wing gives it enough lift to support the airplane.

Bernoulli's principle, then, is another way of saying that for kinetic energy to increase, potential energy must decrease and vice versa.

has air that is under pressure. In this case, the kinetic energy is changed into potential energy of gas pressure.

Air wrenches, air pressure spray paint guns, and air drills all make use of the fact that the potential energy of compressed air can be changed into the kinetic energy of moving air. An air wrench is attached by hose to a tank that has compressed air. When the air is released, potential energy of pressure is changed into the active, spinning energy of the wrench.

Bernoulli's principle states that the velocity of a fluid and its pressure are inversely related. As speed increases, the pressure decreases. The principle is named after Daniel Bernoulli. The simplest demonstration of Bernoulli's principle is to place a small strip of paper below the lower lip and blow. The paper will rise. The fast flowing air reduces the pressure on the upper surface of the paper. On the lower surface, the pressure is unaffected. The paper rises because of the pressure pushing up from below.

Air has both potential energy (energy due to pressure) and kinetic energy (energy due to motion). When air travels faster, it converts potential energy of pressure into kinetic energy

SOLUTIONS

1. Metal springs and struts twist and untwist to smooth the ride.

2. A high water tower produces water pressure.

3. Buoyancy produces a lifting force on an object in a fluid.

As air flows faster, its pressure becomes less.

T F	1.	A rubber band is elastic because it will stretch.
T F	2.	Steel is highly elastic.
	3.	The amount a solid object bends is directly proportional to the _____ acting on it.
A B	4.	Spreading the weight of a solid over greater area (A. increases B. reduces) pressure.
A B	5.	The factor most important in producing water pressure is the (A. height B. volume) of the water tank.
T F	6.	The pressure of a liquid acts equally in all directions.
A B C D	7.	Density is equal to mass divided by (A. area B. pressure C. volume D. weight).
A B	8.	As a hurricane approaches, air pressure will (A. increase B. decrease).
A B C	9.	The rate of diffusion of a gas is inversely proportional to the (A. square B. square root C. sum) of its molecular weight.

Matching

10. _____ Archimedes' principle of buoyancy
11. _____ Boyle's law
12. _____ Ideal gas law
13. _____ Bernoulli's principle

a. Pressure times volume of any gas divided by the temperature is a constant.
b. The lifting force acting on a solid object immersed in water is equal to the weight of the water shoved aside by the object.
c. The velocity of a fluid and its pressure are inversely related.
d. The volume of a gas is inversely proportional to the pressure.

Wave Motion

Waves are an efficient way to send energy from one place to another. Toss a stone into a pond. It makes waves that travel across the water, but molecules of the water move only a short distance. They rise and fall but do not take part in the horizontal motion of the wave. You can see this by watching something floating in the water such as a leaf or chip of wood. The wood goes up and then down, but after the wave passes, the wood is back to very near its original location.

Water waves are transverse. The word means crossways. The disturbance is at right angles to the direction of the wave. A water wave disturbs the surface of the water vertically — up and down — but the wave moves horizontally across the water.

The main parts of a wave are the axis, crest, and trough. The flat surface of the water is the axis. The high point of the wave is the crest, while the low point is the trough. The displacement

PROBLEMS

1. What causes sound?

2. Can sound be reflected?

3. How can birdwatchers use sound to identify a bird?

Can You Propose Solutions?

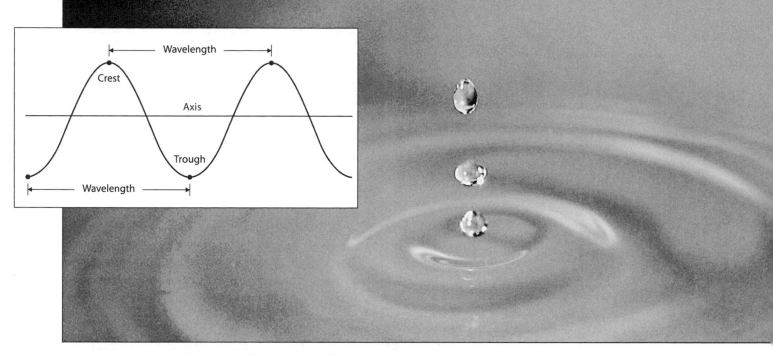

Wavelength measured from crest to crest or trough to trough.

is the distance from a point on the wave to the axis. At a crest or trough, the displacement is at its maximum.

Think about how a piece of floating wood moves as a wave passes. At first it is resting on the undisturbed surface of the water. It is on the axis and its displacement is zero. As the wave passes, the wood rises to the crest, falls back to the axis, and continues into the trough. Finally, it rises again to its beginning level.

Length of a wave includes both crest and trough. The width of a crest is one-half of a wavelength. The width of a trough is one-half of a wavelength. Together they make a full wavelength. Wavelength can also be measured as the distance from one point on a wave to the same location on the next wave. From the crest of one wave to the crest of the next wave is a full wavelength.

Frequency is the number of waves per time interval. Suppose you are standing on a beach and timing waves as they come in. You notice that seven waves lap up on the shore every minute. The frequency is seven waves per minute, 7 wave/min.

In addition to wavelength and frequency, velocity is another property of wave motion. Velocity is the speed at which a wave travels through the medium carrying it. If you tie one end of a rope to a post and then shake

the other end, a wave travels along the rope. The speed is how fast the wave travels from one end of the rope to other, not the speed at which the rope rises and falls.

You can calculate the speed of a wave in the same way you calculate the speed of any other object: divide distance by time. Suppose a water wave takes three minutes (180 seconds) to cross a pond that is a quarter mile (1,320 feet) across. Find speed by dividing distance by time: $v = d/t = 1,320 \text{ ft}/180 \text{ sec} = 7.3 \text{ ft/sec}$.

Physicists have found another way to calculate the speed of waves. Instead of measuring distance and time, they use the frequency and wavelength. The frequency tells us the number of waves made in a set amount of time. The wavelength gives us the distance along the waves. The product of the two quantities gives the total distance the waves travel in that amount of time. The result is the wave equation: velocity = frequency × wavelength.

Suppose you shake a rope so that it makes exactly four waves a second, and each wave is two feet long. Then the velocity of the wave along the rope is eight feet per second: velocity = frequency × wavelength = 4 waves/sec × 2 ft/wave = 8 ft/sec.

The usefulness of the wave equation, velocity = frequency × wavelength, is that

Measure the Speed of Sound

Sound travels so slowly that its speed can be measured with ordinary equipment. Station one person at the end of a football field and beat a drum four times a second. A second person walks down the field but looks at the person hitting the drum and listens for the sound. As the distance increases, the mallet hits the drum, but the sound comes a little later. It arrives late because it has to travel from the drum to the listener. At still greater distance, the mallet hits the drum and the listener hears the sound at the same moment. However, the sound is off by ¼ of a second. The listener is hearing the sound of the previous beat. The distance between observer and drummer divided by 0.25 sec gives the speed of sound. (A drum is not necessary. Two pieces of wood such as short lengths of 2 × 4 lumber can be slapped together to make the noise.)

At 68°F (20°C), the speed of sound in air is about 1,130 ft/sec. The speed changes depending on temperature. Sound travels faster in hot air than it does in cool air.

Sound waves are produced by vibrations — back and forth motions. For sound to be made, something has to be in motion. You speak by vibrating vocal cords in your voice box in your throat. A creaking door makes a noise by the movement of rusty hinges. The sound of wind comes from leaves and branches moving back and forth. To say that something is still is also to say that it is quiet.

When you pluck a guitar string, the string vibrates back and forth. It alternately pushes back and forth on molecules of air. The energy of the vibrating string transmits through the air as the disturbance is passed from one molecule to the next. Although the sound is carried across the room, each individual molecule in the air does not move far. First it is shoved forward, then it is drawn back. Similar to the chip of wood on the pond, each individual molecule of air ends in about the same place after the sound wave passes.

Sound waves do differ from water waves in one important way. Rather than air molecules being moved at right angles to the motion of the wave, sound waves push back and forth on the air molecules in the same direction that the wave travels. Sound waves are longitudinal. The word means lengthwise. The disturbance in the air is in the same direction that the sound moves.

The appearance of sound waves are best described by watching a wave travel along a child's toy known by the brand name of Slinky. A Slinky is a coiled spring. It can be stretched out along the floor and then given a rapid back and forth motion in the same direction as its length. A longitudinal wave travels along the spring. The wave is made of two parts. One part has the coils close together and the other part has the coils widely separated.

In the same way, a longitudinal sound wave is made of two parts. In one part, air molecules are pressed together. They make a region of higher air pressure. The next part has molecules which are more widely separated and give a region of lower air pressure. The distance from the region of greatest compression of one

it works for any wave motion whether it be waves along a rope, water waves, light waves, or sound waves.

wave to the region of greatest compression of the next wave is one wavelength.

The frequency of sound waves is the number of vibrations per second, which for sound is called its pitch. A tuning fork vibrating at middle C makes 256 waves per second. The pitch and frequency is 256 waves per second. A high pitch is also a high frequency. High C is 512 waves per second. Low C is 128 waves per second. (Musicians use slightly different scales than physicists. Musicians set middle C equal to 264 vibrations per second.)

Knowing the velocity of sound (1,130 ft/sec) and frequency of middle C (256 waves/ sec), we can calculate the length of the middle C sound waves. The wave equation, velocity = frequency × wavelength, can be rewritten as wavelength = velocity/frequency. Dividing 1,130 ft/sec by 256 waves/sec gives a wavelength of 4.4 feet.

Human beings can hear sounds in the range of about 20 vibrations to 20,000 vibrations per second. A sound at 20 vibrations per second is an extremely low pitch (low frequency) sound. A sound at 20,000 vibrations per second is an extremely high pitch (high frequency) sound.

The highest pitched sound the human ear can detect is about 20,000 vibrations per second. The waves are but 2/3 of an inch long: wavelength = velocity/frequency = 1,130 ft/sec/20,000 waves/sec = 0.0565 ft/wave, or about 0.678 inches/wave (12 in/ft × 0.0565 ft/ wave = 0.678 in/wave). At the other extreme, the lowest pitched sound that can be heard by humans is about 20 vibrations per second. Those waves are 57 feet long: wavelength = velocity/frequency = 1,130 ft/sec/20 wave/sec = 56.5 ft/wave. It is remarkable to think how well designed the human ear is to detect waves that differ so greatly in their lengths.

A slinky helps us understand the appearance of sound waves by the way it moves.

As people grow older, or if they have been exposed to loud noise over a long time, they lose the ability to hear sounds at each end of the frequency range. Even if you turn up the volume (make the sound louder), they cannot hear very low- or very high-pitched sounds.

The loudness of sound corresponds to the amplitude. The amplitude of a wave is a measure of its maximum displacement from its position of rest. A loud sound causes a greater displacement of the air molecules. They vibrate back and forth over a greater distance around their position at rest.

For a water wave, the amplitude is the distance from the axis to the crest or from the axis to the trough. Toss a pebble gently into water and watch waves. Then vigorously throw a heavy stone into the pond. In the second case, the waves will be bigger. They have greater amplitude than the small ripples.

Changes in amplitude do not change the frequency or velocity of a wave. For instance, a heavy boat that moves through water makes large waves that have large amplitude. A small boat barely moving through the water makes small ripples that have small amplitude. The waves from either boat move at the same speed across the surface of the water. In the same substance, waves travel at the same speed regardless of how they are made or their amplitudes.

Whether you yell or whisper, sound waves travel at the same speed. In air, a loud sound travels at the same speed as a soft sound. The loud sound will travel farther, but it travels no faster than the soft sound.

The frequency at which an object vibrates depends on its length, mass, and tension. You can illustrate some of the ways to change frequency by holding one end of a plastic ruler firmly against the side of a table and flip the end that extends beyond the table. The longer it extends over the edge of the table, the slower it vibrates because of the greater length. If you tape a coin to the free end, the ruler will vibrate at a slower rate because of the increased mass. Tension is important, too. If you replace the plastic ruler with a steel one that has a different tension, the pitch will change.

Stringed instruments also illustrate that length, mass, and tension change the frequency. Look at the strings on a bass, a guitar, and a mandolin. Notice the differences in length, thickness (mass), and tension. They produce different notes because of those differences.

Whenever the entire length of an object vibrates, it produces its natural or fundamental frequency. This is the lowest pitch it can produce. When a string is plucked in the middle, the string vibrates as a whole. It makes its lowest, or fundamental frequency.

At each end where the string cannot vibrate is a node. If you hold a string down in the middle, it has three nodes — one at each end and one in the middle. Between the three nodes are two loops that vibrate separately. Rather than a single fundamental frequency, it vibrates at twice the fundamental frequency. The string may also vibrate in

Sound Intensity Levels

Source	Decibels
Faintest audible sound	0
Rustling of leaves	8
Whisper	10–20
Average home sounds such as the humming of a refrigerator	20–30
Automobile	40–50
Ordinary conversation	50–60
Heavy street traffic	70–80
Jack hammer	90–100
Thunder	110

The intensity range over which the human ear is able to detect and respond to sounds is much greater than the decibel scale suggests. The extreme sounds listed above actually differ in *energy* by a factor of a hundred billion!

The intensity of sound is measured in a unit called a decibel. The table shows the rating, in decibels, of sounds having a great range of intensity.

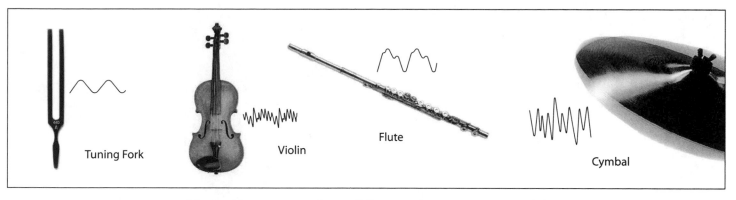

Musical instruments have different vibrations per second.

thirds, in fourths, in fifths, and so on, in simple multiples of the fundamental frequency.

Higher frequency notes are called overtones. An object with its lowest, fundamental frequency of 128 waves/second, will have its first overtone at 256 waves/sec. The second overtone will be 512 waves/sec.

The sound coming from one vibrating object can make other objects vibrate, too. The pedals on a piano release the dampers on piano strings. If you press the pedals of a piano and make a steady note with your voice, you can hear the strings of a similar frequency vibrate in response to the sound waves of your voice.

Resonance occurs when the fundamental frequency of two objects is the same or one vibrates at an overtone of the other. Usually, resonance is demonstrated by holding two tuning forks of the same frequency near one another. When you strike one, alternate high and low air pressures from it strike the other tuning fork and cause it to vibrate, too. Resonance is also known as sympathetic vibration.

Resonance has applications beyond music or sound. For instance, shock absorbers in cars are made of springs that have a certain fundamental frequency. Should the car be driven along a road with an irregular surface that puts the springs in motion in their fundamental frequency, the car can begin a shimmy so violent the driver must slow down.

Resonance does not necessarily require a strong force. Instead, a small force applied at regular intervals can have the same effect. For instance, children on a swing can pump up motion by swinging their legs at the right time. The small motion of the legs can affect the entire motion of the child.

Almost every object that is exposed to wind or other back and forth motion is subject to sympathetic vibration. Bridges and skyscrapers are no exception. Bridges have collapsed and windows have popped out of skyscrapers because of back and forth motion caused by wind. Structural engineers control vibration in the same way that musicians change the fundamental frequency of a guitar string. They change the mass, length, or tension. They use shorter or longer frame members (length), lighter or heavier beams (mass), or looser or stiffer supports (tension).

In changing the fundamental frequency, it is not necessary to make the structure longer, heavier, or stiffer. Sometimes, vibration will cease if the structure is made shorter, lighter, or less stiff.

Automobiles are designed to give a smooth ride at highway speeds. If a driver does stop-and-go driving in the city, the car may vibrate when at stoplights. A mechanic can adjust the idle speed of the engine by a small amount of 50 revolutions per minute either way — faster or slower — to make the vibration go away. The change in engine speed prevents it from vibrating at the same frequency as the frame of the car.

When waves from two different sources meet, they can affect one another. For instance, watch as ripples from two different stones tossed into a pond cross one another. If the crest of one meets the crest of the other, then the wave becomes larger. They reinforce one another. If the crest of one meets the trough of the other, then the waves cancel one another.

Sound waves can interfere with one another, too. Think about sound waves produced by two tuning forks of slightly different pitch. Both are struck at the same time. At first, the two sources of sound waves act together. High pressure meets high pressure and low pressure meets low pressure. The sound is twice as loud, but a few moments later, the tuning fork that vibrates at the slower rate falls behind the other one. Now the high pressure meets low pressure and they cancel one another.

A person listening to the out-of-phase tuning forks will hear a throbbing sound known as a beat. Before the use of electronic tuners, musicians listened for beats to verify that their instruments were in tune.

Waves can be reflected. When they strike an obstruction, the waves bounce back. An echo is reflected sound. At an overlook in front of a canyon wall, you can shout a greeting (Hello!) and will hear a few minutes later the reply (*hello*). In some locations, the echo

As bats fly they emit a high-pitched squeak with a frequency of 40,000 cycles per second or higher that aids them in finding insects.

reflects from other surfaces at different distances, and comes back as a series of sounds of different intensities (*hello*, *hello*, *hello*).

Echoes that mix make a reverberation. An announcement over a loudspeaker in a large auditorium is often difficult to understand. Echoes bounce from the walls and reverberate. Lightning is another example of reverberation. The first time a person hears a nearby lightning strike, they are astonished at the sharp, loud crack. Only when lightning is far away does it make the characteristic rolling thunder sound. Echoes from the ground and clouds cause the rumble of thunder.

Acoustics is the study of sound. Ensuring that sound in a large auditorium is clear and easily understood requires skill. Acoustical engineers design the shape and fixtures in concert halls. They use sound-absorbing curtains, acoustical tile, carpet, and upholstered chairs to prevent "hot" (loud) spots or "dead" (quiet) spots.

Echoes can also be used to measure distance. Sound will travel in water, something that radar will not do. Ships use SONAR (Sound Navigation And Ranging) to measure the direction and distance to underwater objects. An underwater speaker emits a loud ping. The sound reflects from the target and returns to a receiver. SONAR detects schools of fish, reveals shipwrecks on the sea floor, and can identify the composition of ocean sediment.

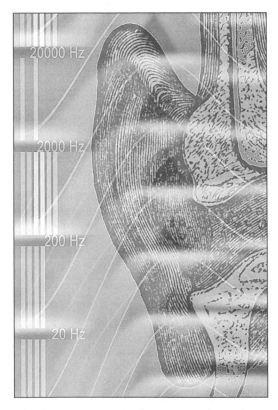

The human ear can hear sounds in the range of 20 to 20,000 vibrations per second.

A sonogram is a view inside the human body produced by sound waves. Soft body parts cannot be seen with x rays, which are only stopped by bones. However, sound waves change speed and direction as they travel through tissues of different densities. Using ultrasonic sound waves can make very accurate images of the insides of the human body.

Higher pitched sounds reflect better because of their short wavelengths. A small wave will reflect from a small object while a large wave will pass over and around it. Sounds with a frequency above 20,000 vibrations per second are ultrasonic. The prefix "ultra" means beyond and "sonic" means sound. Ultrasonic sounds are beyond human hearing. Dogs can hear ultrasonic sounds, and bats can both hear and produce them.

Bats are interested in locating insects. Ultrasonic sounds reflect better than those in the human range of hearing. As bats fly, they emit a high-pitched squeak with a frequency of 40,000 cycles per second or higher. This extremely high-pitched sound has a wavelength of about ¼ of an inch. The wave is so small it will reflect from an insect's body. The bat detects the faint echo and homes in on the insect.

Human vocal cords operate starting at about 100 vibrations per second. We would say that a voice at that pitch is a deep bass. The upper frequency is 6,000 vibrations per second. We would say a person speaking at the upper range has a high soprano voice. The human ear is most sensitive at 2,000 vibrations per second. A faint whisper would be most easily heard at that frequency.

The far left key on a piano keyboard gives a tone of 27 vibrations per second. The right-most key gives a note of a little more than 4,000 vibrations per second. Most musical instruments sound notes somewhere in the range from 25 to 15,000 vibrations per second. However, with one exception, none can make the full range. The exception is the pipe organ. It can make sounds throughout the frequency range that can be heard by the human ear — 20 to 20,000 vibrations per second.

Voiceprint

Voiceprint of American Robin

When bird watching became popular in the 1930s, people began making diagrams of bird-calls to print in books. Each diagram used a series of waves to represent the frequency, loudness, and quality of a bird's song. The diagrams turned out to be fairly simple and allowed identification of each bird by its sound autograph.

Scientists thought it might be possible to show human speech in a similar way, but the human sound-making system is much more complex than that of a bird. In humans, the size of the vocal cavities and the shape and size of the throat, nose, and mouth give sounds a far more complex pattern. Add to this the human ability to move the tongue, jaw, and lips (birds don't have lips) as the sound is made, and the pattern becomes very complex.

However, by 1980, graphs of human speech came into use on a limited basis. The graph of a person speaking became known as a voiceprint. Many people thought voiceprints were as unique as fingerprints, so that individuals could be identified exactly by their voiceprints. However, the ability to represent human voices with a voiceprint has not yet been perfected.

Brightness of light and loudness of sound is a measure of the intensity or energy content of the light or sound. Most human senses do not follow a straight-line response to intensity. Test this yourself by walking from a well-lighted room to the outside on a bright and sunny day. How many times brighter do you think it is? Most people report the change in brightness far less than it actually is. The intensity of a bright day is about 1,000 times as bright as the indoor room. But we do not perceive the difference as that great.

Experiments show that our senses respond by powers of ten. We perceive a light 100 times brighter as only twice as bright. Light that is 1,000 times as bright is perceived as three times as bright. The number 100 is 10^2 and 1,000 is 10^3. It is the exponent, or power, of ten that measures how our senses respond to an increase in brightness or loudness. This powers of ten response is an advantage because our eyes and ears can detect a wide range of intensities.

Sound follows this principle, too. A sound can be 100 times as loud, but we perceive it as only twice as intense. Sound intensity is measured in decibels. The unit is named after Alex-

ander Graham Bell who invented the telephone and also did research on sound and hearing. The unit was originally called a bel. Sounds that differ by 1.0 bel differ in intensity by 10 times. A bel proved to be too large of a unit, so physicists use $1/10$ of a bel, decibel, instead.

The sound of a soft whisper from a distance of three feet is about 10 decibels. The average spoken voice from the same distance is 60 decibels. Traffic on a busy street is 80 decibels. Prolonged exposure to sounds above 80 decibels can permanently damage hearing unless a person wears hearing protection. A sound of about 100 decibels — thunder, for instance — becomes loud enough to be felt as well as heard.

The intensity of a loud sound at 100 decibels (thunder) compared to that of a soft sound at 10 decibels (whisper) is immense. The difference of 90 decibels (100 decibels – 10 decibels = 90 decibels) is equal to 9 bels. Each bel is a power of ten, so the total difference is ten multiplied by itself nine times, 10^9, or 1,000,000,000. Thunder is one trillion times louder than a whisper. Yet our ears are able to hear both thunder and whisper, a remarkable ability.

Sound waves become less intense as they spread out from a source. Sound, like gravity and several other quantities in physics, weaken by the square of the distance. Sound in air expands outward as a sphere. The energy is spread along the surface of the sphere. The surface area of a sphere depends on the square of its radius. A sphere with a radius twice as large has four times the surface area. A sphere with a radius three times as large has nine times the surface area.

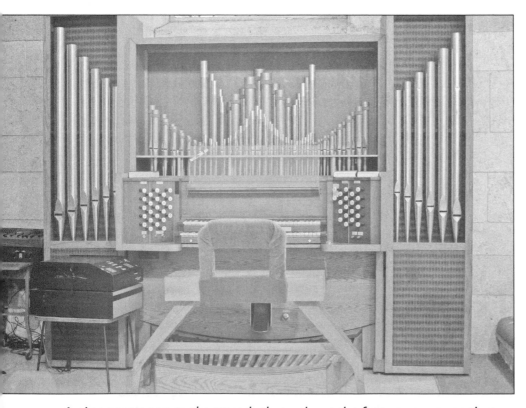

A pipe organ can make sounds throughout the frequency range that can be heard by the human ear — 20 to 20,000 vibrations per second.

In other words, sound intensity varies inversely with the square of the distance from the source. When you move twice as far away from a person talking, the sound becomes only 1/4 as loud. When you move three times as far away, the sound becomes 1/9 as loud.

Actually, sound falls off even more quickly than the inverse square law would predict. Air molecules absorb sound energy. The lost energy is changed into heat.

The inverse square law also fails if sound waves are not free to expand in a sphere. Loudspeakers direct the sound in a specific direction. The sound does not expand in a spherical shell, and for that reason it does not follow the inverse square law.

Quality is the third property of sound. Frequency (pitch) and amplitude (loudness) are the other two. Quality is the fundamental frequency and the number and prominence of overtones. A tuning fork, violin, and piano can play the same note, but the source is easily identified. A tuning fork plays at a fundamental frequency with practically no overtones. A violin has a range of overtones that give it a wavering quality. A piano has quality between that of the violin and tuning fork.

Each person has a unique voice because of the quality. The throat, mouth, and nose give overtones to the sound made by the vocal cords. Because no two individuals are identical, each voice differs in quality.

Electronic instruments can sound like different musical instruments because physicists have learned how to identify pitch, amplitude, and quality of different instruments. They use a process developed by a French mathematician named Joseph Fourier. In 1822, long before electronic music had been invented, Fourier showed that even the most complex wave motion could be represented by a series of simple waves. The process is called Fourier analysis.

Every sound, no matter how complex, is a combination of a main tone (pitch), overtones (quality), and amplitude (loudness). Fourier analysis takes sounds made by musical instru-

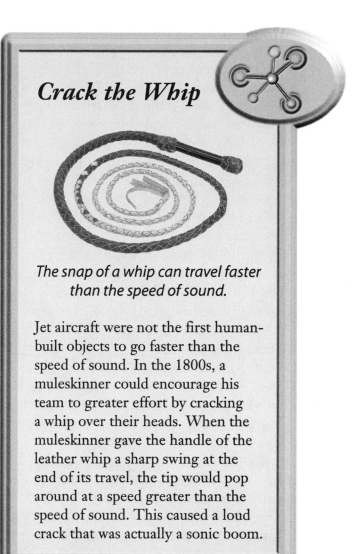

Crack the Whip

The snap of a whip can travel faster than the speed of sound.

Jet aircraft were not the first human-built objects to go faster than the speed of sound. In the 1800s, a muleskinner could encourage his team to greater effort by cracking a whip over their heads. When the muleskinner gave the handle of the leather whip a sharp swing at the end of its travel, the tip would pop around at a speed greater than the speed of sound. This caused a loud crack that was actually a sonic boom.

ments and identifies the number, prominence, and frequency of the overtones. An electronic music synthesizer then creates these same frequencies to sound like a drum, piano, violin, or other instrument.

The human ear is capable of Fourier analysis. When a room is filled with conversation, a person can listen and understand a single individual. We can listen to a complex mix of sounds, separate the components, and then interpret the parts that pertain to the on-going conversation from a single individual. This is but one example of the intelligent design of the human body.

Sound waves travel at the same speed in air regardless of their source. This is contrary to our everyday experience for other motions.

Normally, two velocities are added together if they are in the same direction. For instance, if a person throws a ball forward from a moving car, the ball's speed is equal to the speed at which it was thrown and the speed of the car. A ball thrown forward at 20 mi/hr from a car going 60 mi/hr will have a speed of 80 mi/hr. (Of course, air resistance will quickly slow it down.)

The velocity of sound is different. In air, sound travels at about 1,130 ft/sec. Sound a whistle from the window while traveling in a car at 60 mi/hr (about 88 ft/sec). Does the sound go faster by 88 ft/sec? No. Once the sound waves leave the whistle, they travel at 1,130 ft/sec in all directions, both forward and backward from the car.

Although velocity does not change, frequency does. Waves in front of a moving source are crowded together. This gives them a shorter wavelength and higher frequency. Those waves behind the moving source separate and have a greater space between them. This gives them a longer wavelength and lower frequency.

For thousands of years, the change in frequency went unnoticed because the speed of travel was too slow to make it apparent. In the 1800s, people noticed the sound of a locomotive whistle as the train passed the station. As the train approached the sound was higher pitched than it would be if the train were stopped. As the train passed, the pitch became lower.

Christian Doppler (1802–1853), an Austrian physicist, worked out the mathematical formula relating the pitch to the motion of source and observer. Suppose a horn makes a sound that has a frequency (pitch) of middle C, 256 waves/sec. For a train going 60 miles per hour (88 ft/sec), Doppler's equation predicted the sound would be 278 waves/sec as it approached and 231 waves/sec as it pulled away. That was a very noticeable difference in frequency.

Doppler tested his equation by having a locomotive pulling a flatcar pass through a crossing at different speeds. On the flatcar, musicians played trumpets at a fixed note. Other musicians listened at the crossing as the train passed. The musicians confirmed that Doppler's calculations were correct.

The change in frequency of wave motion because of motion of the source or observer is known as the Doppler effect. The Doppler effect applies to all wave motion: sound, water, waves, or light. Either the source of the waves or the observer may be in motion. When combined motion of source and observer brings them closer, pitch is higher. When motion separates them, pitch is lower.

As a source of sound goes faster and faster, the waves in front of the vehicle crowd closer and closer together. As aircraft fly at the speed of sound or faster, the sound waves they produce are crowded together in a shock wave that forms a cone with its tip at the nose of the plane. A sonic boom sweeps across the ground below the plane.

SOLUTIONS

1. Vibrating objects make sound.

2. Reflected sound is an echo.

3. A bird's song can be shown as a voiceprint picture.

The sound an object makes depends on its length, thickness, and tension.

T F   1.   Waves are an efficient way to send energy from one place to another.

A B C D   2.   The distance along a wave including crest and trough is its (A. axis   B. frequency   C. velocity   D. wavelength).

A B   3.   The number of waves produced per time interval is its (A. frequency   B. velocity.)

A B C   4.   Dividing how far a wave travels by the time it takes to travel that distance gives the wave's (A. frequency   B. velocity   C. wavelength).

5.   The speed of any wave can be found by multiplying its frequency by its _____.

T F   6.   Sound is produced by back and forth motion.

A B C D   7.   The frequency of a sound is known as its (A. amplitude   B. color   C. pitch   D. velocity).

A B   8.   The maximum displacement of a wave from its position of rest is its (A. amplitude   B. wavelength).

A B   9.   A loud sound has (A. high   B. low) amplitude.

T F   10.   A loud sound travels faster than a soft sound.

11.   The pitch of a string on a stringed instrument depends on the length, thickness, and _____ of the string.

A B   12.   The (A. highest   B. lowest) pitch an object can make is known as its natural or fundamental frequency.

A B C D 13.   The study of sound is known as (A. acoustics   B. astronomy   C. mechanics   D. thermodynamics).

A B   14.   High frequency, ultrasonic sounds reflect (A. better   B. worse) from small objects than low frequency sounds.

A B   15.   We perceive a light 100 times brighter as (A. 100 times   B. twice) as bright.

A B C D 16.   The loudness of sound is measured in (A. candles   B. decibels   C. joules   D. watts).

T F   17.   As sound waves spread out, they grow weaker by the square of the distance.

18.   The three properties of a sound are frequency, intensity, and _____.

A B   19.   Sound waves travel at the (A. same speed   B. different speeds) in air depending on their source.

A B   20.   If pitch increases, then source and observer must be moving (A. toward   B. away from) one another.

Chapter Nine

Light

Our world is filled with light and color. We watch color televisions, wear colorful clothes, and read books with colorful pictures. Long ago, most people wore brown, gray, or white clothes. Only rich kings could afford clothes colored red, blue, or purple with costly dyes, but everyone could enjoy the rainbow, which was one of the most colorful sights in their lives.

The rainbow is an interesting sight for us today. You may have seen a rainbow after a summer rainstorm. Thousands of raindrops separate sunlight into colors. On the outside of the rainbow you see red, then orange, yellow, green, blue, indigo, and finally violet on the inside.

What causes the colors? The first scientist to investigate the rainbow carefully was the English scientist Isaac Newton. While still a student at Trinity College he decided to study the nature of light and color.

PROBLEMS

1. Is sunlight pure and colorless?

2. How does the eye see all colors?

3. Is the speed of light the same in all substances?

Can You Propose Solutions?

Newton's experiment with a glass prism shows that by mixing all the colors you get white light.

On rainy days, Isaac rushed outside to look for a rainbow. On frosty nights, he stayed up to measure the halo around the moon. He even filled a pipe with soapy water and blew soap bubbles. He peered closely at the colors that shone on the surface of the bubbles.

For centuries, natural philosophers (as scientists were called then) had argued about the nature of sunlight. Some scientists thought that sunlight, which they called white light, was pure and colorless. They said, "The prism colors the light as it passes through the prism."

Newton disagreed. A glass prism was perfectly clear. So were drops of rain. He believed sunlight had the colors all along. Isaac grew weary of reading the many conflicting theories about light and color. "A single experiment carried out carefully is worth a dozen books filled with guesses."

He bought a prism, which is a piece of clear glass shaped like a solid triangle. Sunlight flashing through the triangular piece of glass threw out a vivid rainbow. Isaac called the pattern of colored lights a spectrum.

In a dark room, he let a small beam of sunlight through a hole in the window blind. The ray passed through his prism and a rainbow fell upon a screen. Most scientists thought that these colors were created inside the prism. Next, he turned a second prism around and passed the rainbow through it. The second prism put the colors back together. They made a spot of white light on the screen.

Newton's experiment showed that mixing all colors gave pure, white light. All colors of the rainbow go into making sunlight, or any white light that looks colorless. Rather than being without color, white light has all the colors in equal amounts.

We see light and color with our eyes. The human eye has been compared to a camera, and the eye and camera do have some features in common. However, the eye is a special creation of God and is in many ways far more adaptable to extreme conditions than a camera. As the brightness of a late evening scene fades, our eyes automatically switch to black and white vision. Then in deeper darkness a special

Rainbow

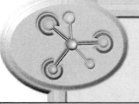

A rainbow can be seen in raindrops after a rainstorm has passed. It is always found on the other side of the sky from the sun. Stand with your back to the sun and face the rain cloud. The sun must be low in the sky. Look for a rainbow early in the morning or late in the day. On a bright day, two rainbows are visible. One is below the other. We usually see a rainbow as a small part of a circle. From a high mountain or in an airplane, we can see the entire circle of a rainbow.

chemical, visual purple, allows us to see objects 100,000 times dimmer than they were in bright daylight.

The outer bulge of the human eye is the cornea. It acts as a convex lens to bring light to a focus. A convex lens is thicker in the middle than at the edges. When rays of light pass through a convex lens they are brought to a focus. A magnifying glass is a convex lens. Like the convex lens of a magnifying glass, the cornea is shaped to bring rays of light to a focus and form an image on the retina at the back of the eye.

Behind the cornea is the iris that can open or close to change the amount of light that enters the eye. The iris is the colored part of the eye — blue, brown, gray, black, or green.

The pupil is the opening in the center of the iris where light enters the eye. In very bright light, the iris closes down so the pupil is only about 1/12 inch (about two millimeters) across. But in dim light, the iris opens so the pupil is about 1/3 inch (about seven millimeters) wide. The amount of light entering the eye depends on the area of the pupil. Area is directly related to the square of the diameter. Twelve times as much light enters the eye in dim light as in bright light: $7^2/2^2 = 49/4 = 12$ approximately.

The cornea, like other convex lenses, has a position where it brings light to best focus. You can use a magnifying glass to show how the cornea makes an image. A room with the lights off and one small window works best. Stand near the wall with the window on the other side. Hold a magnifying glass so light from the window passes through the magnifying glass. Move the magnifying glass back and forth until it forms a clear image on the wall. The image will show best against a white sheet of paper. The image is upside down.

The magnifying glass forms what is called a real image. A real image is one that can be projected onto the wall or some other surface such as a screen or piece of paper. The image is upside-down because rays of light from the top of the window go through the magnifying glass and end up on the bottom of the image.

The magnifying glass must be moved back and forth so it is the right distance from the screen to produce a sharp image. Like the magnifying glass, the cornea would make clear images only of objects at a certain distance. Objects too close or too far would appear blurred. Yet, most people can clearly see objects only ten inches from the eye all the way out to distant objects.

Another part of the eye, the lens, allows the eye to focus on both near and far objects. Unlike the cornea, the lens can change shape. The lens is found behind the iris. The lens is held by muscles that contract or relax, causing it to become thinner or thicker. The lens become more sharply curved to see near objects or less sharply curved to see far objects.

The lens adjusts what part of the image is in clear focus. Look up from reading a book and out a window at a distant scene. The lens in your eyes automatically changes shape so that the area of clear focus switches from the book 15 inches from your eyes to the distant scene that is several hundred feet away.

The cornea and lens work together to clearly focus an image on the retina, a surface of nerves called rods and cones. These nerves are sensitive to light. Nerves of the retina leave the eye through the optic nerve and carry messages that the brain interprets.

Rods are especially sensitive to light, but cannot tell different colors. In dim light, rods provide vision, but we see objects in black, white, or gray.

Cones see colors. For a long time, color vision puzzled scientists. The rainbow is made of several different colors. The colors change smoothly from red to orange, from orange to yellow, from yellow to green and so on. And between red and orange is a reddish orange. In fact, rather than seven colors of the spectrum, there are an immense number of colors, each differing only slightly from the other. Does the eye have nerve endings (cones) to detect each of the different colors?

James Clerk Maxwell, a Scottish physicist, was the first scientist to develop an understanding of color vision. He grew up in the 1800s in Scotland. As a child, his father gave him an interesting toy. A circular sheet of paper attached to a wheel had drawings of a dog jumping through a hoop. Each drawing was slightly different from the previous one. James looked through slits in the wheel as it spun and saw the drawings reflected in a mirror. The dog appeared to be doing its trick.

James and his cousin, who was a good artist, drew other displays such as the lifecycle of a tadpole. Once they accidentally colored a particular part of the drawings red but colored the rest green. When James spun the wheel, he saw yellow instead of red or green. No one could explain why he saw a color that wasn't there.

Because of his never-ending interest in light and color, James Maxwell watched changing patterns of light. He bobbed his head this way or that at light shining through glasses of water and gazed fascinated at colors sparkling from cut glass ornaments. His fellow students called him Dafty because of his strange behavior.

While in college, James Maxwell built an improved version of the wheel he had played with as a child. He fitted together a red disk and a green disk so that half of each showed. When he rapidly turned the wheel, he saw neither red nor green but yellow.

Many scientists believed that the eye had to have nerves, called receptors, for each color. James Maxwell's experiments showed that the eye could not tell the difference between pure yellow from the sunlight and yellow made by combining red and green. He experimented with other color combinations. James concluded that, "We see colors because of red, green, and blue receptors in the eye. However, light is not limited to just those three colors."

Light was the first thing created by God. Scientists have spent centuries trying to understand light and color vision. Many unanswered questions still exist. For instance, James investigated colorblindness. He discovered that most colorblind people could not tell the difference between red and green. A way to overcome this condition has yet to be developed.

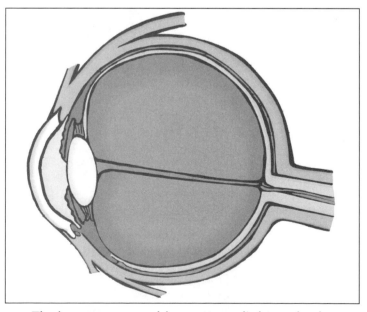

The human eye enables us to see light and color.

Cones are of three types. One type sees red, another sees green, and the third type sees blue. If light triggers only one type of cone, then we see only that color. When the eye forms an image of a red car on the retina, then only the red cones respond and our brain tells us the car is red.

We see the full range of colors because an in-between color causes two types of cones to respond. For instance, yellow has a wavelength that is a little shorter than red light but a little longer than green light. Yellow light affects some red cones and some green cones. Signals from both the red and green cones at the same time causes the brain to interpret the color as yellow.

Suppose a spotlight of red light is aimed on a screen. Then a spotlight of green light is aimed so it strikes the same screen and overlaps the red. In the overlap, the eye sees yellow, although yellow is not in either spotlight.

Mixing red, green, or blue light in the right amounts can make the eye see all other colors. Instead of sending out all of the colors

in the rainbow, a television station sends out only three signals for red, green, and blue. On the television screen, the complete range of colors is visible to the eye. Examine a television screen up close and you will see tiny dots, each one some shade of red, green, or blue.

Because of their important role in color vision, scientists call the colors red, green, and blue primary colors. They are known as additive primary colors because if all three colors are added together they give white light. Suppose beams of red light, green light, and blue light are projected at the same spot on a screen. The three colors mix together to give white light. The three additive primary colors are sometimes abbreviated RGB, for **R**ed, **G**reen, and **B**lue.

Normally, light travels in straight lines. When a person rides a bicycle down a narrow path, the bicycle rider relies upon the common observation that light travels in a straight line. If the bicycle path looks straight, then the rider assumes it is straight. Rays of light can

Mirages are optical illusions caused by the refraction (bending) of light.

Subtractive Primary Colors

Artists make colors by mixing paints called pigments. Artists have a different set of primary colors: cyan, magenta, and yellow. Cyan is a mixture of green and blue. Magenta is a mixture of blue and red. Yellow is a mixture of red and green.

The primary colors that artists use are called subtractive primary colors. Suppose an artist needed to paint a green pepper but had no green pigment. The artist could make green by mixing cyan and yellow. Cyan removes — subtracts — all colors but blue and green. It reflects only those two colors. Yellow removes all colors but red and green. It reflects only those two colors. Mix cyan and yellow. The eye sees only green because that is the only color that both paints reflect.

Artists make new colors by mixing pigments.

Sometimes artists call the subtractive primary colors blue (cyan), red (magenta), and yellow. Scientists and artists use different primary colors and different names for the colors. When scientists and artists talk to one another about primary colors, it can be confusing.

Colored pictures in books and magazines use subtractive primary colors. So do photographs from color printers connected to personal computers. Tiny dots of cyan, magenta, and yellow ink are put on white paper to produce color images. Black ink is often used, too, because when pigments are mixed to give black, they sometimes give a muddy brown. The black ink makes a darker black. The subtractive primary colors are abbreviated CMYK, for **C**yan, **M**agenta, **Y**ellow, and blac**K**.

reflect from mirrors or have their paths bent by lenses.

When light does not follow that everyday rule of straight-line travel, our sense of vision can be fooled. An optical illusion is an image that misleads the eyes. A mirage makes a person think water is in the distance but it is not really there. A mirage forms on a hot day. A layer of hot air refracts (bends) rays from the blue sky. The shimmering blue image of the sky on the surface of the land looks like the surface of a lake.

David Livingstone, the great African explorer, once crossed the Kalahari Desert. He and the people with him ran out of water.

Then, off in the distance, they saw the welcome sight of a lake. They threw down their packs and ran across the desert. As they topped a rise and dropped down into the lake they found nothing but sand. Only later did they find an oasis with real water.

A mirage can sometimes fool our eyes. But the bending or reflecting of light also makes possible eyeglasses, contact lenses, and magnifying glasses so we can see better. Lenses in microscopes, binoculars, telescopes, and cameras produce images because the mirrors and lenses in them change the direction of light.

Reflection is a change of direction in light. Suppose you were to throw a ball against a

Reflection

A mirror can fool animals that do not normally see their own reflection. A grouper is a type of fish. It claims an area along the sea bottom and keeps out other fish. If a mirror is put in its territory, the grouper will attack its own reflection. It sees what it thinks is another fish and tries to run it away. The grouper's image appears to be behind the mirror, although nothing is actually there.

wall. The ball will go in at a certain angle and then bounce away at the same angle. Suppose you put a mirror on the wall and replaced the ball with the beam of light from a flashlight. The ray of light would make exactly the same path as the ball. Light always bounces away from a mirror at the same angle that it came into the mirror. This fact is known as the law of reflection.

Because a mirror may be curved as well as flat, scientists do not measure the angles from the surface of the mirror. Instead, they use a line that is perpendicular to the surface of the mirror at the point where the ray reflects. This line is called a normal. It makes a 90-degree angle with the surface of the mirror. The law of reflection states that the angle a ray makes with the normal going into a mirror is equal to the angle the reflected ray makes with the normal.

In addition to real images that can be projected onto a screen, images can also be virtual. A virtual image appears to be in a location where it cannot actually exist. A flat mirror gives a virtual image. When you look into a flat mirror, your reflection appears to be behind the mirror, although the mirror may be hung on a solid wall. The image is virtual because the rays of light that make the image come from in front of the mirror and are not actually behind the wall.

A mirror can be curved rather than flat. Isaac Newton used a concave mirror to build a telescope. A concave mirror has the shape of the bowl part of a spoon. It is scooped out in the middle. Such a mirror can form a real image. Like a convex lens, a concave mirror can take light from a distant object and bring it to a focus.

Isaac Newton's telescope became known as a reflecting telescope because it used a mirror to reflect light to a focus. In his telescope, the main mirror was at the bottom of the tube. Light rays traveled the length of the tube and struck the concave mirror. The rays reflected toward a focus at the top of the tube. Before coming to a focus, a small secondary flat mirror reflected the rays through an opening in the side of the tube. The image formed outside the tube. The astronomer then used a type of magnifying glass, called an eyepiece, to magnify the image still more.

Most large modern telescopes today use a concave mirror to gather light and form an image of outer space objects. A small telescope with a main lens two inches in diameter collects about 70 times as much light as the eye alone. The size of a telescope refers to the distance across the main mirror, not the length of the tube. An amateur astronomer who says he has a 12-inch telescope means that it has a mirror 12 inches across. The tube would be about eight feet long.

The United States has a national observatory on Kitt Peak near Tucson, Arizona. The largest telescope there has a convex mirror that is 13 feet (4 meters) across. Astronomers usually put their telescopes on high mountains to be away from haze and air pollution. Kitt Peak is 6,882 feet high. An observatory at the summit of Mauna Kea on the big island of Hawaii

The national observatory on Kitt Peak was built at this location because telescopes need to be above haze and air pollution to see great distances. Kitt Peak is 6,882 feet high.

is at 13,796 feet — more than two miles. In 1990, the Hubble Space Telescope was given the best location of all. With an orbit 600 miles high, it was far above the atmosphere of earth.

Telescopes are made to gather light as well as give a magnified view. Many objects in space are hard to see because they are dim. Some binoculars are made for night vision. The lenses are big and gather more light. It is as if you had pupils two inches across. The binoculars gather 70 times as much light as your eyes alone. Telescopes with large mirrors collect thousands of times as much light as our eyes.

Rather than being concave, a mirror can be curved so that it bulges out like a Christmas tree ornament. It is a convex mirror. One advantage of a convex mirror is that it gives a wide field of view. Some stores have convex mirrors so the store clerk at the register can see the entire store. School buses have these mirrors so the driver can see that young children are not out of sight at the front of the bus.

Automobiles also have gently curved mirrors to improve the field of view. The driver can see objects that would otherwise be hidden. However, a convex mirror forms a smaller image than a flat mirror and it appears to be farther away. Convex automobile mirrors have a written warning that objects are closer than they appear.

Binoculars, microscopes, magnifying glasses, and some telescopes use lenses rather than mirrors to bring light to a focus and form images. The main lens is convex. It is thicker in the middle than at the edges. Convex lenses came into use about 800 years ago to help people read small print. A convex lens is also known as a reading lens.

When held next to the eye, a convex lens lets a person's eyes focus closer than normal. An object viewed through the lens appears larger than normal. The magnification of a simple reading lens depends on its focal length. A sharply curved lens with a short focal length

The First Microscope

Anton Leeuwenhoek was not a professional scientist. He had practically no training in science. He lived in Delft, Holland, in the 1600s. He ran a store that sold cloth and sewing supplies. By trial and error he found that very sharply curved magnifying lenses with extremely short focal lengths gave an enlarged view of tiny objects.

Anton's microscope revealed new living organisms.

It took exceptional skill to grind and polish these delicate little lenses. Although no larger than the head of a pin, Anton's lenses gave sharp and clear images. One of Anton's lenses magnified 270 times.

Along with patience and keen eyesight, Anton possessed a never-ending curiosity. He peered at everything with his microscopes. He examined hair, skin, cork, ivory, blood, wings of insects, scales of fish, muscle tissue — everything. Often, he found detail no one had seen before. He carefully described what he saw and made detailed drawings.

He examined insects and noticed that a fly's vision came from 4,000 eyes, each with an individual lens. Starting in 1673, he began sending letters to the Royal Society in London. The Royal Society was an important scientific organization. Although Anton had only an elementary school education, members of the Royal Society asked him to keep on telling them about his discoveries.

In 1674, Anton made one of the greatest scientific discoveries of all time. He found a world of living things inside a drop of canal water. The little living things seemed to be everywhere — in water in rain barrels, ponds, and the canals of Holland. It was a truly unexpected finding. He watched them in fascination. They moved, ate, grew, and reproduced. Anton's microscope revealed that living tissue was far more complex than anyone had imagined.

magnifies more than one less steeply curved with a longer focal length.

Focal length is a measure of how far it takes for a lens to bring parallel rays of light to a focus. The easiest way to find the focal length is to find an object that is very far away, such as a distant street light or the sun, and then bring its light to a focus. The distance from the lens to the image is the focal length. Most magnifying glasses have a focal length of three to six inches.

The magnifying power of a simple lens is based on two distances. One is the closest distance a person can comfortably focus. For most people this is about 10 inches (25 cm). The other is the focal length of the lens. Magnification is given by dividing the close focus distance by the focal length. If a magnifying glass has a focal length of four inches, then it will make an object appear 2.5 times life size: 10 inch/4 inch = 2.5 x. The x stands for magnification. A jeweler who examines a diamond uses a more powerful lens. It has a focal length of about one inch (2.5 cm.) The magnification is 10 in/1 in = 10 x.

Most modern microscopes use two lenses. One forms an image and the second one magnifies the image. The magnification is given by multiplying the effect of the two lenses together. Most microscopes used in schools have a lens that makes an image 10 times larger than the object being viewed. The eyepiece then magnifies the image another 10 times. The total magnification is $10 \times 10 = 100$.

In 1850, Jean Foucault, a French physicist, measured the speed of light in a vacuum as well as in other transparent substances such as air, water, and glass. He found that light slows when it enters air, water, glass, or other substances. The speed of light in water is much slower than in air, and slower still in glass. In a vacuum, its speed is 186,000 miles per second, in water it slows to 140,000 miles per second, and in glass its speed is about 124,000 miles per second. Light travels slowest in diamond. Its speed is only 78,000 miles per second (126,000 km/sec).

When light goes from air into glass it changes speed. If it enters at an angle, it also changes direction. To understand why, imagine four friends who walk with their arms interlocked across a sidewalk and onto a sandy beach. The first one to step into the sand walks more slowly. This causes the others to be pulled around. One by one, they step into the sand. Not only do they go slower, but they also change course. In the same way, when light enters a glass at an angle, it goes slower and its path is bent.

Refraction is the bending of light when it goes from air to water or some other more dense substance such as glass. You can see refraction by putting a pencil against the side of a glass partially full of water. The pencil looks like it bends where the water begins.

Another example of refraction of light can be seen with a large glass aquarium tank filled with water. When viewed from one side, the far side looks closer than it really is. Look into

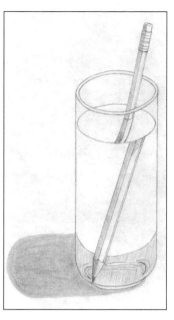

Refraction can be seen by putting a pencil in a glass filled with water.

the tank from above. The bottom of the tank seems closer than when the tank is empty of water. If the water is very clear, a tank three feet deep will appear to be only two feet deep.

Light goes about 50 miles per second slower in air than in a vacuum. Even the slight difference in the refraction of air and a vacuum becomes visible at sunset. When the sun is directly overhead, it enters the atmosphere at 90 degrees and the rays are not refracted, although they do slow down slightly. At sunset, the rays enter the atmosphere at almost 90 degrees and refraction bends the rays so the image of the sun stays visible longer. From the time the lower edge of the sun first touches the horizon to the moment its upper edge disappears from sight should take two minutes. Because of refraction, the event

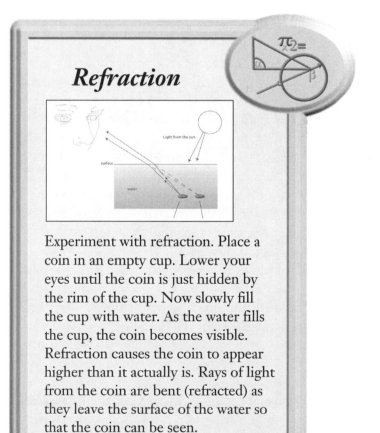

Refraction

Experiment with refraction. Place a coin in an empty cup. Lower your eyes until the coin is just hidden by the rim of the cup. Now slowly fill the cup with water. As the water fills the cup, the coin becomes visible. Refraction causes the coin to appear higher than it actually is. Rays of light from the coin are bent (refracted) as they leave the surface of the water so that the coin can be seen.

Light for Communication and Computing

Scientists are working today to make new inventions that use light and color. Light waves can carry more information than radio waves. Telephone companies use small glass fibers rather than wires to carry thousands of telephone messages. Computer scientists are experimenting with computers that use beams of light to make calculations at the speed of light.

takes six minutes. The sun seems to hang on the horizon. It is actually visible after it has passed below the horizon.

Sunlight reaches the earth through the vacuum of space. Light is a wave, but a special kind of wave. Most waves need something to carry them. Sound waves usually travel through air. Water waves are carried along the surface of water. Light is a type of wave that needs nothing to carry it.

Light is made of electromagnetic waves. They have an electric part and a magnetic part. They can travel through a vacuum.

A light wave is small. Like a water wave, a light wave has a high part called the crest and a low part called the trough. A complete wave includes both the crest and trough. The length of a water wave is measured in feet. But light waves are many times smaller. It takes 50,000 light waves placed end to end to be one inch (25 mm) long.

Sound and visible light do differ considerably in the size of their waves. A sound wave with a pitch of middle C (256 vibrations per second) has a wavelength of about 4.4 feet (1.34 meters). Light has a wavelength of about 0.0002 inches (0.005 millimeters). A sound wave is well over two million times longer than a light wave.

Frequency and wavelength of any wave motion vary inversely to one another. As the frequency increases, the wavelength decreases. The frequency of sound is its pitch. As the pitch increases, from low C to middle C to high C, sound waves get shorter and shorter.

For visible light, higher frequency light has shorter wavelength. The frequency of light is its color. The highest frequency and shortest waves that human eyes can detect are violet. The lowest frequency and longest waves that the human eye can sense are red. Red light has waves that are about twice as long as waves of violet light. The other colors have waves that are shorter than red light but longer than violet.

Light has always been a surprising subject. When scientists think they understand it, new facts show that they still have much to learn. For instance, light sometimes acts not as waves but as tiny bundles of energy called photons.

SOLUTIONS

1. Sunlight has all the colors of the rainbow.

2. The eye has but three color receptors (red, green, and blue) but can detect all colors.

3. Light slows as it enters water, glass, or other substances.

Light can travel in a vacuum.

Matching

1. _____ brings light to a focus.
2. _____ controls the amount of light that enters the eye.
3. _____ is the opening through which light enters the eye.
4. _____ adjusts light to the best focus.
5. _____ is a surface of light sensitive nerves.
6. _____ carries information from the eye to brain.
7. _____ is sensitive to light but cannot see color.
8. _____ is sensitive to light and can distinguish color.

   a. Cones
   b. Cornea
   c. Iris
   d. Lens
   e. Optic nerve
   f. Pupil
   g. Retina
   h. Rods

T F   9. Sunlight is a mixture of all the colors of the rainbow.

10. The eye has cones that can detect red, green, and _____ light.

A B   11. The observation that light bounces from a mirror at the same angle at which it enters is known as the law of (A. reflection B. refraction).

A B   12. The image behind a flat mirror is a (A. real B. virtual) image.

A B   13. Most modern, large telescopes use a (A. lens B. mirror) to collect light and bring it to a focus.

A B   14. A lens thicker in the middle than at the edges is (A. convex B. concave).

A B   15. The speed of light is (A. faster B. slower) in water than in air.

A B   16. The bending of the sun's rays at sunset is an example of (A. refraction B. reflection).

T F   17. The frequency of light is its brightness.

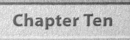

Chapter Ten

Electricity

Thales of Melitus, a Greek scientist, lived about 600 years before Christ. He reported that when he stroked amber with wool, the amber would pick up feathers or straw. Amber is hard, fossilized tree sap. Amber could be given a charge of static electricity. The words electricity and electron are from the Greek word for amber, elektron.

More than 2,000 years passed. In the 1500s, William Gilbert, an English physician, showed that substances other than amber could have an electric charge. Amber was used to make jewelry, so he tested other gemstones, too. He rubbed diamonds, opals, and sapphires with fur. They gained an electric charge.

He also experimented with magnets and realized that magnetism came in two different types. There was a north-seeking magnetic pole and south-seeking magnetic pole. He wondered if electricity came in two different

PROBLEMS

1. What causes static electricity?

2. Which is weaker, static electricity or gravity?

3. How can energy be sent through wires?

Can You Propose Solutions?

types, too, although he could not find a way to decide one way or another.

A French scientist named Charles Du Fay believed electricity came in two different types. He made one type by rubbing amber with wool. He made the other type by rubbing glass with silk. Both types would attract a cork ball held by a thread. Then he touched the cork with the charged glass to give the cork the same charge as the glass. The charged glass now repelled the cork. However, amber would attract the cork. According to Charles Du Fay, glass had one type of charge and amber another type of charge.

Benjamin Franklin, the American scientist, disagreed that electricity had two forms.

He visualized electricity as a fluid that flowed because of friction of rubbing. A charged object either had too much of the fluid or too little of the fluid. Franklin used plus sign, +, to show an excess of the fluid and minus sign, −, to show a shortage of electricity.

Which idea was correct? Later experiments proved that electric charge does have two forms. One type is carried by the proton, which has a positive charge. The other type is carried by the electron, which has a negative charge. However, Benjamin Franklin was partially correct. Protons are at the center of the atom and are not free to move from place to place. Electrons are located on the fringes of atoms, and in some substances they can move about freely.

Benjamin Franklin

printed a yearly calendar called *Poor Richard's Almanac*.

When in England he had developed an interest in science. Isaac Newton lived in London at the same time he was there. Franklin's study of heat led him to build a cast iron stove that sat out in a room and was more efficient at heating than a fireplace. The Franklin stove became a common way to cook and heat in the Colonies and in Europe, especially as coal and wood came into shorter supply.

Franklin's electrical experiments began in 1747. He sent letters about his experiment to friends in England who read them before the Royal Society. Franklin became famous throughout Europe as America's first important scientist. He was elected to the Royal Society.

From 1757–1775 Franklin represented the Colonies in England. As British rule grew more oppressive, he saw independence from England as the only solution. In 1776, Franklin helped draft the Declaration of Independence and signed the document.

Benjamin Franklin was the 15th child of 17, born to a poor candlemaker. He attended only two years of school. He worked first for his father and then for his brother, a printer. In 1723, at age 17, he struck out on his own.

The next year, a Philadelphia storeowner sent him to England, but the storeowner did not give him enough money, so he could not afford passage back to America. Franklin worked for a London printing firm. He lived in England for 18 months before he could come home. In Philadelphia, Franklin opened his own print shop. He started a newspaper and

Electrical Fields

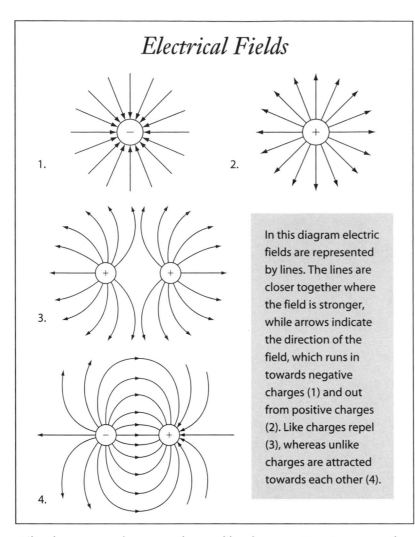

In this diagram electric fields are represented by lines. The lines are closer together where the field is stronger, while arrows indicate the direction of the field, which runs in towards negative charges (1) and out from positive charges (2). Like charges repel (3), whereas unlike charges are attracted towards each other (4).

Like charges repel one another; unlike charges attract one another.

An object with a negative charge has more electrons than protons. An object with a positive charge has more protons than electrons. A neutral object has an equal number of protons and electrons. Usually, an object becomes charged because the electrons enter or leave the object.

Benjamin Franklin continued to experiment with electricity. He put together facts that others had discovered and added new information. He developed the three laws of static electricity. (The word static means "at rest.")

First, he noticed that charged objects such as glass or amber would attract small pieces of paper, feathers, hair, or lint. Uncharged objects are attracted equally well to objects with static charges. It does not matter whether the charge is positive or negative.

Next, he suspended two charged glass rods from strings and brought them near one another. The glass rods, each with a positive charge, repelled one another. The same occurred when two objects with a negative charge were brought near one another. He concluded that like charges repel one another.

Finally, he brought a glass rod that had a positive charge near a rubber rod that had a negative charge. They attracted one another. He concluded that unlike charges attract one another.

In 1776, the year the American Colonies declared their independence, Charles Coulomb, a French engineer, began a series of delicate experiments to measure the force of attraction between two charged objects. He proved that the force of attraction, or repulsion if they are like charges, followed the inverse square law. If two charged objects are moved so they are twice as far away, the force between them is only $1/4$ as great. If they are separated three times as far, the force between them is only $1/9$ as great.

Charles Coulomb developed the law of static electric force. It states that the force between two electrically charged objects is directly proportional to the product of their electric charge and inversely proportional to the square of the distance separating them. Coulomb's law of static electric force is very similar to Newton's law of gravity, but with charge replacing mass.

Which is stronger, gravity or static electricity? Coulomb's law of electrostatic force and Newton's law of gravity make it possible to compare the two forces. Two electrons have the same mass and the same charge. If they are the same distance apart, will they be attracted by their gravity or repelled by their like charge? When scientists do the calculations, they find that the electric forces are vastly greater than the gravitational attraction. Electrostatic forces are about 10^{42} times greater. That is 10 followed by 42 zeros! It is not that electric forces are so strong, but that gravity is so weak. Gravitational force is by far the weakest force known in nature.

Electricity can be at rest; that is, static electricity. Some substances are good at holding a static electric charge. These substances include crystals, glass, resin (hard tree sap), and plastic. They are given an electric charge by rubbing them with fur, wool, or silk. Because they hold a charge and do not let it go, they are called nonconductors. The best nonconductors are nonmetals. Nonconductors include glass, minerals such as mica, and rubber.

Atoms of a nonconductor have all of their electrons fixed in place. The protons hold them tightly. For electricity to flow, electrons must move from atom to atom. If none of the electrons can move, then the electricity cannot flow. It is like a room of people with all the chairs taken. No one will get up because they might lose their seats.

Diagram of a copper atom. Copper is an electrical conductor because one of the electrons from a copper atom can break free and travel along a copper wire.

Scientists who first began experimenting with electricity had a problem. They could not touch the wire carrying electricity or let it touch other metals. If they did, the electricity would escape. They needed something to insulate the wire. They discovered that dry silk is a nonconductor. They wrapped the wires with silk ribbon.

Today, rubber or plastic coats wires. The rubber and plastic are electrical insulators.

Insulators are nonconductors used to keep electrons flowing within conductors.

The opposite of an insulator is a conductor. Current electricity can pass through a conductor. The word current means "to flow."

Electric current flows through circuits in devices all around you. You flip a switch and lights come on in your room. Your clock shows time. A toaster, microwave, or stove cooks food. Bells ring at school. Game machines, music players, and televisions entertain you. In all of these devices, electricity follows a path called an electrical circuit.

A circuit is a complete path that an electrical current can flow around. A circuit has a source of electricity and at least one device that uses the electricity.

A flashlight is an example of an electrical circuit. Batteries in the handle of the flashlight supply the electricity. Wires make a path for electricity to the light bulb. Along the way, a switch lets you turn on or off the flow of electricity. If the switch is on, electricity causes the light bulb to glow. The electricity then completes the circuit by going back along the wires to the other end of the batteries.

Electricity that flows in a wire is made of electrons. Some atoms have a large number of electrons. At least one of the electrons has a path that takes it far from the positive charge that holds it. An outside force can give it a shove and cause it to break away from the atom. A battery provides the force that puts electrons in motion in a circuit.

The Lunar Rover (on right) was powered by electricity

still weigh less than a copper wire.

In our daily use of electricity, we use electric current. Current is measured in amperes, abbreviated amps. It is named in honor of Andrè Ampére, a French scientist. He was the first to measure the current in a wire. It takes a lot of electrons to make one ampere. A total of 6,250,000,000,000,000,000 electrons (a little more than six billion billion electrons) must pass through a circuit every second to make one ampere of current.

Most metals allow electricity to flow easily. Copper, silver, and aluminum are examples of metals. A copper atom has 29 protons and 29 electrons. One of the electrons has a path that takes it far from the protons. It can break free and travel along a copper wire. For that reason, copper is called an electrical conductor.

All metals are conductors, although some are better than others. Silver is the best conductor. It is a shiny white metal. Because silver is so costly, it is seldom used to make electrical wires.

Copper is the second best conductor. It is not as expensive as silver. Copper is often used to make wires that are found in radios, telephones, televisions, and the wires that go from the battery in flashlights, but even it is too expensive when wires have to run long distances.

Electric power stations that generate electricity are often far from the cities where the electricity is used. The electricity is carried from the source to the city by cross-country highline wires. Rather than copper, these wires are made of aluminum because it is cheaper and lighter than copper. An aluminum wire can be made larger to carry more electricity and

The amount of current that a battery can provide depends on its size. Some game machines and music players take AA size batteries. (Others have internal batteries that can be recharged.) An AA battery can supply about two amperes of current. The battery does not produce two amps of current in one second. Instead, it gives a much smaller amount of current but over several hours.

We normally think of batteries as being used to power small devices, but many of the first automobiles ran on batteries. They were made in the late 1800s. People liked them better than cars with gasoline engines. Gas engines had to be started by turning a crank by hand. The engine made a lot of noise. The first gasoline engines needed frequent repairs. Electric cars had fewer problems. They started by pushing down on a pedal that made electricity flow. They ran quietly. They seldom needed repairs.

Electric cars had a top speed of about 30 miles (48 km) per hour. They could only go 50 miles (81 km) on a full charge. Recharging took all night. Battery-powered cars slowly lost favor. Cars that ran on batteries alone quit being made in 1930.

Electric cars for special uses continued to be built. Electric golf carts are practical for short trips where the driver stops often. They are used on golf courses and other places. People who keep parks clean use them to collect trash and carry garden tools. Battery-powered vehicles do not give off smoke or fumes. They haul cargo inside buildings such as warehouses.

The Lunar Rover was an unusual electric car. In 1971, astronauts on the moon drove around in one. The Lunar Rover was about the same size as a golf cart, 10 feet (3.0 m) long and 43 inches (1.1 m) across. It had seats for two astronauts. Electric batteries gave the Lunar Rover a top speed of nine miles per hour.

Some bicycles and special personal transportation devices such as the Segway are battery powered.

Recently, carmakers have developed hybrid cars. A hybrid car has both an electric motor and a gas engine. The gas engine is smaller than most car engines. It runs at a set speed that gives the best gas mileage. A hybrid car does not have to be plugged in at night to charge the batteries. Instead, the gas engine recharges batteries when extra power is not needed.

An electric motor helps when the hybrid car needs to speed up quickly or go up steep hills. When the car slows, the energy of braking turns the electric motor in a reverse direction. This generates electricity rather than uses it, and the extra energy is put back into the batteries. Some hybrid cars go about twice as far on a tank of gas as a regular car.

Electrons in a metal need a push to get them moving. The push is called voltage. Voltage is named after Count Volta of Italy. He was the first to make an electric battery.

Batteries have their voltage written on them.

Count Allessandro Volta

Voltage is the force that pushes electrons around a circuit. A small voltage gives electrons a gentle shove. A high voltage gives electrons a stronger shove. A small voltage can send electricity through a good conductor such as a copper wire. If the voltage is high enough it can cause electrons to spark across a nonconductor such as dry air. A small 1½ volt battery can send electrons around a wire, but 25,000 volts is needed to cause electrons to jump across a one-inch gap in dry air.

Batteries have their voltage written on them. A single flashlight battery, called a cell, makes 1.5 volts. Other batteries are 6 volts or 9 volts. Batteries in cars are 12 volts.

The household current in the United States is 110 volts. In other parts of the world, a voltage of 220 is used. The push of voltage is needed to overcome resistance in an electric circuit. Resistance acts against the motion of electrons.

Current, resistance, and voltage are related to one another. Georg Simon Ohm was the first scientist to discover how they are related. He taught high school science. He built his own equipment to experiment with electricity. Most of his discoveries were minor ones. In addition, because he did not teach at a well-known university, most of the discoveries he did make were ignored at first.

He found that simple rules described the flow of electricity through wires. For instance, current flow is directly proportional to voltage. The greater the voltage, the greater the current.

The flow of electricity can be compared to the flow of water through a pipe. A fire hose can spray a lot of water on a burning building in a short amount of time. The pump is

Electric Messages

As a young man, Samuel F.B. Morse (1791–1872) studied painting in England. He wrote home to his parents, "I only wish you had this letter now. But 3,000 miles are not passed over in an instant." Morse returned to the United States. He became a successful artist.

In 1832, Morse visited France. On the return voyage, he heard that electricity in a wire traveled as fast as lightning. He tested whether electricity could be used to send speedy messages. Morse invented the telegraph. The word telegraph means "writing at a distance." His invention did not impress businessmen. No one would buy it.

Finally, after 12 years of trying, Morse built a test line between Washington, D.C., and Baltimore, Maryland. The first official message was "What hath God wrought!" But an assistant had earlier sent Morse a test message. The Whig party met in Baltimore to name a person to run for president. Morse's assistant flashed the fact that Henry Clay had been chosen. Reporters rushed by train to Washington with the news. But a Washington newspaper already had the headline sent by telegraph: "The Ticket Is Clay!"

Samuel Morse

For electricity, a battery or electric generator is the pump. The pressure produced is the voltage. A voltage of 3.0 volts sends twice as much electricity through a circuit as 1.5 volts. For homes, a heavy-duty air conditioner may need a lot of current to operate. It may use 220 volts. Higher voltage forces more electricity through the wires.

Ohm discovered that resistance is another factor that controls the flow of electricity. Current and resistance are inversely related. As resistance increases, the current decreases. Ohm found that resistance is directly proportional to the length of a wire. A wire ten times as long has ten times the resistance. Only $1/10$ as much current flows.

A thick wire lets more electricity through. Ohm found that the current-carrying capacity depended on the cross-sectional area of the wire. The size of a wire at the end is its cross-sectional area.

Area is directly proportional to the square of the diameter. So if a wire is twice as thick, then it carries four times as much electricity: $2^2 = 4$. If it is three times as thick, then it carries nine times as much electricity: $3^2 = 9$.

Ohm's most important discovery was that current is directly proportional to voltage

Modern Light Bulb

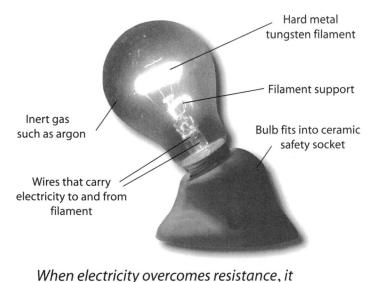

Hard metal tungsten filament

Filament support

Bulb fits into ceramic safety socket

Inert gas such as argon

Wires that carry electricity to and from filament

When electricity overcomes resistance, it produces heat or light.

powerful. It generates pressure that forces the water out quickly. The amount of water that flows in the hose is directly proportional to the pressure produced by the pump.

The Flow of Voltage from a Power Station to Offices and Homes

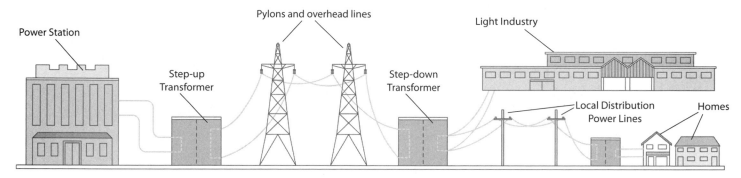

A typical power station generator produces alternating current at 2,400 volts. This is stepped up to hundreds of thousands of volts to reduce the energy loss during long-distance transmission. A main substation step-down transformer reduces the voltage for the local area. Smaller substation transformers reduce it further for distribution to offices and homes.

and inversely proportional to resistance. The discovery, known as Ohm's law, is the fundamental law of electric circuits. Ohm's law can be stated as an equation: current = voltage/resistance.

Although several years passed, scientists finally realized the importance of his work. The unit for measuring resistance, ohm, is named in his honor. He was appointed professor at the University of Munich.

Usually, when electricity overcomes resistance, then it produces heat or light. For example, a light bulb has a small, coiled wire that has high resistance. The wire is called a filament. When electricity flows through the filament, the metal gets so hot it glows. A bread toaster works in the same way. When electricity flows, wires with high resistance in the toaster get hot and glow. The heat toasts the bread.

Electricity is a convenient way to transfer energy from one place to another. Scientists have discovered that some energy is lost because electric current heats wires through which it travels. Heat energy in long-distance electrical transmission lines is wasted energy.

Can the wasted heat energy be reduced? Yes, heat depends on the current but not upon voltage. If the current is reduced, then the heat will be reduced. How can you reduce

current and still transmit the same power? The solution is to increase voltage.

Power is a measure of how quickly work can be done. Electric power depends on both current and voltage. For instance, using the water in the hose as an example, water from a fire hose can knock down a damaged wall because it not only delivers a lot of water, but it also does so with a lot of pressure.

The generator at an electric power plant produces electricity at 2,400 volts. Before the electricity leaves the plant, a step-up transformer increases the voltage from 2,400 volts to 400,000 volts or more. High voltage reduces the number of electrons (current) but gives each electron more power. By increasing the voltage, current can be reduced, and the wires do not get as hot. Less wasted heat is generated.

The disadvantage is that high voltage electricity is extremely dangerous. Like lightning, it can jump from the wire to strike a nearby object. Electricity at 400,000 volts can jump about one foot (30.5 cm) through dry air. It can spring across even greater distances in damp air.

Wires that carry high voltage electricity are strung from tall metal towers. The wires are high above anything that might touch them. The wires are held by insulators to keep them

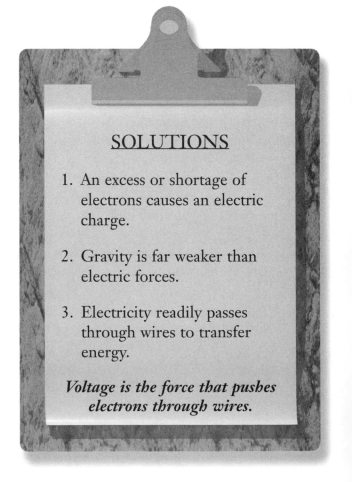

High voltage wires are held by insulators to keep them from contacting the tower.

from contacting the tower. Glass and ceramics are used as electrical insulators.

Voltage is reduced to a safer level when the electricity reaches the city. A step-down transformer changes the voltages back to 2,400 volts. Wires on poles along city streets carry electricity at 2,400 volts. Before going into homes, step-down transformers reduce the voltage yet again. Most homes use electricity at 110 or 220 volts.

Electricity is transmitted cross-country at high voltage to reduce heat lost, but used at lower voltage with greater safety.

Stepping Up or Down

The change of voltage in a transformer depends on the number of turns in the two coils, called the primary and secondary windings. If the secondary has more turns than the primary, voltage is increased (stepped up). If it has fewer, voltage is decreased (stepped down). As voltage rises, current falls, keeping the overall electrical energy the same.

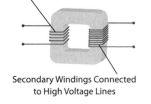

Step-up Transformer

Primary Windings to Electricity Source

Secondary Windings Connected to High Voltage Lines

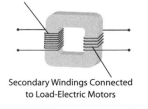

Step-down Transformer

Primary Windings to Electricity Source

Secondary Windings Connected to Load-Electric Motors

Generators at a modern power station do not produce electricity at sufficiently high voltage for efficient transmission. Their voltage is increased by step-up transformers for efficient long-distance transmission.

SOLUTIONS

1. An excess or shortage of electrons causes an electric charge.

2. Gravity is far weaker than electric forces.

3. Electricity readily passes through wires to transfer energy.

Voltage is the force that pushes electrons through wires.

T F   1. Thales of Melitus discovered that amber could be given a charge of static electricity.

A B   2. The one that moves more freely is the (A. electron   B. proton).

T F   3. An object with a positive charge has more protons than electrons.

         4. Coulomb's law of static electric force is very similar to Newton's law of gravity, but with _____ replacing mass.

A B   5. The stronger force is (A. electrostatic   B. gravity).

A B   6. Glass is an example of a (A. conductor   B. nonconductor).

T F   7. All metals conduct electricity.

T F   8. No practical use has been found for battery-powered vehicles.

A B C D   9. The force that pushes electrons around a circuit is (A. resistance   B. charge   C. current   D. voltage).

         10. State Ohm's law:

A B C D 11. The ohm is a unit for measuring (A. current   B. power   C. resistance   D. voltage).

         12. To reduce the heating effect of electricity in wires, the current is reduced but the _____ is increased.

Magnetism

More than 2,500 years ago, Greek scientists discovered a magnetic iron ore in Turkey. The iron ore was named magnetite because it came from a province in Turkey called Magnesia. The mineral would attract pieces of iron. When they suspended magnetite by a string, it pointed in a north-south direction. Magnetite became known as lodestone. The word means leading stone. The first compasses were made of lodestone.

Starting in the 1200s, navigators began using a magnetic compass to guide a ship at sea. They made an iron needle magnetic by stroking it with lodestone. They made the first compasses by placing the magnetized needle on a float in a bowl of water so it could turn freely. Later, they placed the needle on a pivot. The end of the needle that pointed north was called the north-seeking pole, or simply the north pole, N. The other end was the south-seeking pole, or simply the south pole, S.

PROBLEMS

1. What attracts a compass needle?

2. What is the cause of magnetism?

3. Can magnetism be used to make electricity?

Can You Propose Solutions?

Sailors did not entirely trust the compass. The direction the needle pointed along shore often disagreed with true north as marked on charts. The compass sometimes went into wild gyrations, swinging back and forth for no apparent reason.

For centuries, scientific understanding of the compass and magnetism was a fog of ignorance and misinformation. Scientists of that time claimed that all regular and dependable scientific laws originated in the heavens. They believed the perfect action of stars in the northern sky controlled the action of the compass needle. When the compass gave a bad reading, they blamed the sailors rather than the compass.

Scientists taught that garlic would wreak havoc with the magnetic properties of a compass. The British navy took the story seriously. Helmsmen who came on duty with garlic breath were subject to flogging.

A London physician named William Gilbert was the first to separate some of the myth from facts. Being from a merchant family, he believed that despite their lack of formal education, skilled craftsmen had great practical knowledge. He listened to ideas about magnetism from surveyors, navigators, and compass makers.

William Gilbert was well educated. He attended the University of Cambridge and took 11 years to earn his medical degree. This was followed by a four-year, grand tour of Europe. Finally, he settled in London in 1573 and became a respected physician. He served as the court physician for Queen Elizabeth I.

In his spare time, he devoted his efforts to understanding the mystery of magnetism. He traced the statement about garlic affecting lodestone back nearly 1,500 years to a book written by Ptolemy, a Greek astronomer. The

Gilbert discovered that a compass points north because the earth is a magnet. This is an example of a dip compass.

story was repeated but never tested in all of that time.

William Gilbert suspended a lodestone from a thread and let it hang freely. The lodestone promptly rotated until one end faced north. Gilbert chewed on raw garlic until his breath carried a pungent odor. He breathed on the lodestone. It held a true north-south course. He even smeared a compass needle with garlic juice. Its properties were not harmed. He decided, "The whole thing is fable and hearsay."

Gilbert tested other superstitions. Some people purchased a magnetic cap to wear to cure them of headaches. His tests showed the whole idea a waste of money.

Although scholars believed the compass was drawn toward the North Star, no one had found a way to test this claim. One of Gilbert's friends was Robert Norman, a compass maker. Norman built a compass with a needle that was free to point up and down.

Gilbert purchased the special compass. When he released the needle, he expected it to rise and point toward Polaris, the North Star. To his astonishment, it pointed down. It aimed for a point below the horizon thousands of miles away from London.

He carved a miniature earth out of a large lodestone. He moved a compass along the surface of the miniature earth. It pointed in the same direction as a real compass going around the real earth.

"The compass points north because the earth is a magnet," Gilbert said in wonder. "One pole is somewhere in the Arctic and the other pole is in the Antarctic."

The little magnetic model of the earth allowed him to solve another mystery. Mariners reported confusing variation in the

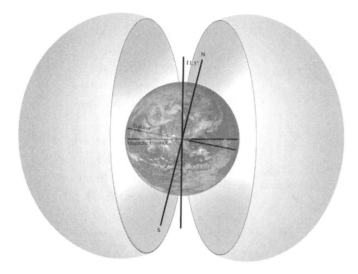

The Earth's magnetic and geographic poles are usually at slightly different locations.

direction the compass pointed when their ships came near shore. Gilbert speculated that mountains along the shore pulled the compass off course. He gouged out valleys on his miniature earth, and confirmed what he had guessed. Magnets are pulled off course by minerals in mountains.

By explaining the science of the compass, Gilbert removed some of the superstitious fear of its use. Navigators took longer sea voyages.

In 1600, Gilbert published a summary of 18 years of his magnetic researches. His method of research in which he tested ideas by experiments influenced scientists such as Galileo, Kepler, and Newton.

For years after Gilbert's book was published, scientists thought earth's magnetic field was fixed in place. However, the earth's magnetic poles move about from year to year. The movement is so great that once every 10 years, maps and charts are updated to take into account the new location of magnetic north.

Storms on the sun also affect the compass. These storms shoot charged particles into space. Particles wash over the earth. The upper atmosphere glows to produce the Northern Lights. The particles cause violent changes in the earth's magnetic field. Compass needles undergo sudden, wild changes. Imagine how frightened

seamen of the 1400s would become if the compass needle suddenly began swinging wildly.

The space around a magnet where it exerts its attractive or repulsive force is its magnetic field. One easy way to trace out a magnetic field is to place a magnet under a piece of paper and then sprinkle iron filings over the paper. Tap the paper slightly and the iron filings will align with the magnetic field. The lines will be tightly packed together at the north pole and the south pole, but will spread out from each of the poles.

The iron filings curve around the magnet along lines of force. The region around the magnet where it attracts iron or acts upon other magnets is its force field. Iron filings reveal the direction of the force field. The magnet is strongest where it has many lines that are close together. The field can be mapped even better with a compass. It aligns itself along the magnetic lines of force.

The earth rotates on its axis, and at each end of the axis are the geographic poles of the earth. A compass points to magnetic north, which is about 1,100 miles away from the geographic North Pole. The magnetic pole in the southern hemisphere is located between Antarctica and Australia, west of Ross Sea. It is about 1,200 miles from the south geographic pole.

The distance between the two gives rise to errors in the direction that a compass points. The difference between the direction of a geographic north and magnetic north is known as magnetic variation. In Massachusetts, a compass points about 15 degrees west of geographic north. In northern California, on the other side of the United States, a compass points about 15 degrees east of geographic north. Charts for sailors and maps for hikers are marked with this difference. The hiker then adds or subtracts the difference to find true north.

The earth's composition, especially minerals in mountains, can cause a compass to have a local error. In certain parts of the Rocky

Mountains, the north end of a compass actually points south.

It is interesting to contrast and compare the attraction due to gravity, static electricity, and magnetism. Gravity is a far weaker force than electrical or magnetic ones, but gravity acts upon any substance and not merely bits of fluff or pieces of iron.

The force of gravity follows the law discovered by Isaac Newton: the force of attraction between any two objects is directly proportional to the product of the masses of the two objects but inversely proportional to the square of the distance separating them. Massive objects attract one another more strongly than less massive objects. The farther they are apart, the less the attraction, and the force weakens by the square of the distance. Objects four times as far away attract with a force only $1/16$ as great.

Gravity only attracts. No experiment has ever produced an example in which gravity acts as a force that repels. Unlike gravity, static and magnetic forces can either attract or repel.

Static electricity occurs in two forms: positive static charge and a negative static charge. The force of static electricity follows a law very similar to that of the law of gravity. The force of attraction between two objects with a static charge is directly proportional to the product of their charges but inversely proportional to the square of the distance separating them.

An object can carry a single static charge without a corresponding opposite charge. Scientists can isolate a single negative charge from a group of electrons or a single positive charge from a group of protons. For instance, amber can carry a negative charge without having a corresponding positive charge.

Magnets, however, always have a north pole and a south pole. A bar magnet has a north pole at one end and a south pole at the other end. If it is cut in half, this does not separate the poles. Instead, each half now has north and south poles. No scientist has succeeded in making a single north pole without a corresponding south pole. However, making a very

Draw a Magnetic Field

A bar magnet shows the magnetic fields of the magnet and the earth.

You can plot a magnetic field with a small compass. First, put a bar magnet on a sheet of paper. Then put a compass at one of the poles. Place a dot on the sheet of paper at the head of the compass needle. Move the compass so the tail of the needle is on the dot. Now mark the next dot for the head of the needle. Repeat to follow its curving course around to the other pole of the magnet.

You are plotting the effect of two magnetic fields. One belongs to the bar magnet. The other belongs to the earth. If the bar magnet is placed along the lines of force of the earth's magnetic field (north and south), then the line of force plotted by the compass will smoothly curve around and return to the other end of the bar magnet.

If the bar magnet is not placed along a north and south line, then the earth's own magnetic field will affect the compass. If the compass path carries it too far from the bar magnet, the earth's magnetic field may take over. Rather than returning to the other end of the bar magnet, the path of the compass may instead curve away and follow a line of force that belongs to the earth's magnetic field.

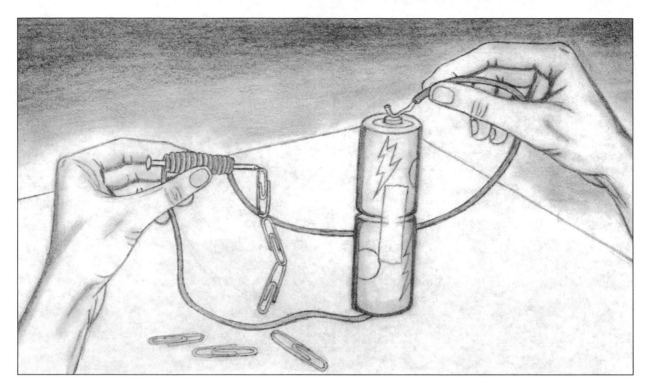

Paper clips temporarily take on a magnetic force when hooked to a battery.

long bar magnet can simulate a single magnetic pole. Although two poles are still present at each end of the bar, they are so far apart that the effect of one upon another is greatly weakened.

Magnets also differ from gravity and static electricity in what they attract. Gravity attracts anything. Static electricity attracts light objects such as feathers or pieces of paper. Magnets affect only a few types of metals.

Magnets strongly attract ferromagnetic metals. Iron is the best-known ferromagnetic metal. Others include nickel, cobalt, and alloys that contain them. If an iron bar is placed near a magnet, the lines of force from the magnet will change direction to travel through the iron bar. The magnet's lines of force travel better in iron than in air.

Magnets weakly attract paramagnetic metals. Aluminum and magnesium are examples of paramagnetic metals. Lines of force from a magnet curve to enter aluminum, but not as strongly as they do to enter iron.

When paramagnetic elements are combined with ferromagnetic metals, they produce alloys that are strongly attractive and make powerful permanent magnets. Alnico is one of the strongest ferromagnetic substances known. It is an alloy of iron, aluminum, nickel, and cobalt. The word alnico is made of the chemical symbols for aluminum, Al; nickel, Ni; and cobalt; Co.

Magnets weakly repel a third class of metals. These metals include gold, silver, and copper. Lines of force change direction to avoid going into gold. They travel better in air than in gold.

Like static electricity, there are three laws of magnetism. First, either pole of a magnet will attract a nonmagnetic metal such as iron. Second, like magnetic poles repel one another. Third, unlike magnetic poles attract one another. A north pole of one magnet will attract the south pole of another magnet but repel the north pole of that same magnet.

The force of attraction of magnetism also follows a law similar to the law of gravity and static electricity. The force of attraction or repulsion between poles of any two magnets is directly proportional to the product of the strength of their magnetic fields and inversely proportional to the square of the distance separating them. Charles Coulomb, the French scientist, not only established the law of static electricity, but also proved this law for magnetism in 1785.

Scientists have learned that magnetism is due to the motion of electric charge. Each electron that whirls in its orbit around the nucleus of an atom is a tiny electric current, and it generates a miniature magnetic field. Most electrons occur in pairs that orbit in opposite directions. Their magnetic fields cancel one another.

Atoms of iron and other ferromagnetic substances have electrons orbiting alone in their outer electron level. Overall, each atom has a magnetic field around it caused by these unpaired electrons.

The magnetic field of an individual iron atom is so strong that atoms next to it turn their magnetic field in the same direction. Iron atoms cluster together in groups called magnetic domains. Each domain is a tiny magnet. Although small, magnetic domains can be seen in a microscope.

All ferromagnetic substances have magnetic domains. An iron bar is filled with domains, but they are pointing every which way. Because they are not aligned, the domains neutralize one another. In pure iron, known as soft iron, the domains can switch around easily.

If a bar of soft iron is put in a magnetic field, the domains shift around so they align with the magnetic field. The soft iron then becomes a temporary magnet, but when the magnetic field is removed, the magnetism disappears from the soft iron. Soft iron makes a temporary magnet because even at room temperature, heat causes motion in the domains. They become jumbled, work against one another, and the magnetism is lost.

For instance, when you touch a magnet to iron paperclips and pull it away, paperclips come along. Domains in the metal of the paperclip align with the magnetic field and the paperclip becomes a temporary magnet. The first paperclip becomes a temporary magnet and attracts the next one. The second one becomes a temporary magnet and attracts the next one. Sometimes a chain of five or more paperclips comes up with the magnet. If you pull the first one away from the magnet, it loses its magnetism and those below it fall away. The domains of the first paperclip become disorganized. It loses its magnetism, and so do those attracted to it.

Steel, an iron alloy, has domains that are more difficult to align. However, once they do become aligned, the effect is permanent. Steel can be made into a permanent magnet. The first compass needles were of steel that had been stroked in the same direction for 50 to 100 times until the domains became aligned.

The magnetism of any magnet, even a permanent one, can be lost if the domains get jumbled and lose their alignment. Heat is one way to destroy magnetic properties. When a

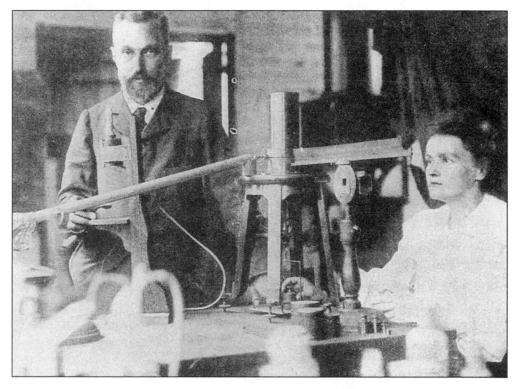

Pierre Curie discovered that magnetism can be lost through heat. In this photo he is in the lab with his wife, Marie Curie.

Everyday Uses of Permanent Magnets

A horseshoe magnet is U-shaped. Putting the north and south poles near one another makes the magnets stronger. It can lift heavier objects. Police sometimes tie ropes to horseshoe magnets and use them to raise from lake bottoms objects used in crimes.

Grazing cattle sometimes swallow small pieces of wire and other bits of iron that could injure them. Farmers feed them cow magnets — strong, smooth, rounded bar magnets. Cow magnets lodge in the first chamber of their stomachs and attract the iron to keep it safely out of their digestive tracts.

Most refrigerator doors are held closed with magnets. The strip around the door is a flexable magnet. The frame around the refrigerator is also magnetic. When the door is closed, the magnets attract one another and form a tight seal. Most refrigerator doors are also home to magnets that hold notes, pictures, small calendars, and other magnetic items.

Telephones use magnets, as do the speakers in televisions, radios, and music players. Credit cards have a small

A horseshoe magnet is a type of permanent magnet.

magnetic strip on the back that contains information.

All airplanes, regardless of their modern navigation equipment, are required to also have a regular magnetic compass. The compass is very similar to the one used by ships' captains of 300 years ago. Should the airplane's electrical systme fail, the magnetic compass would continue to show the plane's heading.

ferromagnetic substance is heated to a certain temperature, it abruptly loses all of its magnetism. For iron, this temperature is 1,455°F (791°C). Heat causes the domains to wiggle around so they no longer work together.

The temperature at which magnetism is lost is the Curie temperature. It is named for Pierre Curie who discovered this property in 1895. (He and his wife, Marie Curie, also discovered the radioactive element radium.) Metals with low Curie temperatures quickly

and easily become temporary magnets. Those with high Curie temperatures are more difficult to become magnetic, but once they do, they make good permanent magnets.

Another way to damage a magnet is to jar it. Dropping a magnet on a concrete floor, hitting it with a hammer, or any other hard mechanical action violently jars the domains and jumbles them. The magnetism is lost.

The third way to weaken a magnet is to place it near another one, but in such a way that their magnetic fields counter one another. If two magnets are stacked so north pole is to north pole and south pole is to south pole, their mutual repulsion will disarray the domains and weaken both magnets. Magnets should be stacked north pole to south pole. The magnets reinforce the orientation of the domains.

Although permanent magnets have many uses, electromagnets are even more useful. Electromagnets use electricity to make a magnetic field.

Scientists noticed the similarity in laws governing electricity and magnetism. Magnetism had two poles (N, S); electricity had two charges (+, −). Like magnetic poles repelled one another as did like electric charges. Unlike magnetic poles attracted, as did unlike electrical charges. Both followed the inverse square law — their strength decreased by the square of the distance.

However, scientists did not at first discover a connection between magnetism and electricity. Eventually, they concluded that magnetic and electric fields were not related. Most of the scientists had tested static electricity and magnetism.

Electric batteries, invented in 1800, could produce a flowing electric current. Scientists tested an electric current and whether it generated a magnetic field. However, they made a basic error. Wind fills a sail when it hits the sail straight in; that is, at right angles to the sail. Scientists tested an electric current by putting the wire at right angles to a compass needle. When the current flowed, nothing happened. The compass needle did not move. They concluded, once again, that electricity and magnetism were unrelated. One did not have an effect upon the other, they thought.

In 1819, Hans Christian Oersted, a Dutch physics teacher, set up an experiment for his class to show that an electric current had no effect upon a compass needle. In the experiment, however, the wire lay along the compass needle rather than at right angles to it. When a student switched on the electric current, the compass needle flipped to one side and pointed east-west rather than north-south. Oersted could hardly contain his excitement. Oersted and his students had made an important discovery.

When Oersted disconnected the wires from the battery, the compass needle returned to its normal position. He reversed the direction of the current, and the needle flipped around again, but this time in the reverse direction from the earlier experiment.

Oersted proved that an electric current does produce a magnetic field. The magnetic field circles the wire rather than running parallel to it. Suppose a wire is sent vertically through a piece of cardboard. The magnetic lines of force make concentric circles around the wire. The magnetic field is a series of nested circles with the wire in the center.

Scientists quickly began experimenting with magnetic fields produced by

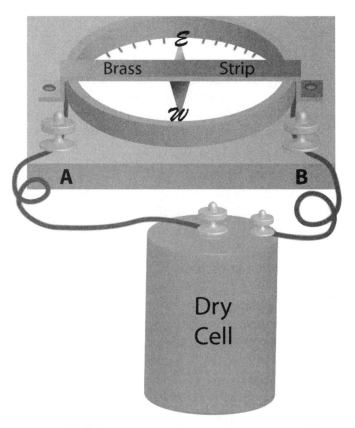

Hans Christian Oersted's experiment proved an electric current produces a magnetic field.

A telegraph uses electromagnets.

current-carrying wires. William Sturgeon of England discovered that wrapping several turns of wire around a soft iron bar would strengthen the magnetic field. In 1823, he built the first electromagnet. It could lift a nine-pound iron weight. Over the next ten years, Joseph Henry, a scientist in the United States, greatly improved on Sturgeon's design. He wrapped hundreds of turns of insulated wire around a central iron core and built a magnet that could lift more than a ton.

Unlike natural magnets, Joseph Henry could control the strength of an electromagnet. It grew stronger with more current and weaker with less current. In addition, he could turn the electromagnet on and off. Without electricity, the soft iron core lost its magnetism. In this way, a heavy load could be lifted and when the electricity was switched off, the load dropped to the ground. Scrap metal dealers and iron smelters used Joseph Henry's strong electromagnets to lift scrap iron and separate iron from crushed iron ore.

Joseph Henry also made tiny magnets whose operation needed but the slightest of currents. In one experiment, he strung a mile long wire from his laboratory to his home. When he turned on the switch and electricity flowed, it operated an electromagnet that rang a bell in his home. He would signal his wife when he started home.

People who wanted the latest technology installed electric doorbells run by batteries.

Doorbells were the first practical use of electromagnets in the home. Samuel F.B. Morse built a telegraph that used an electromagnet to raise and lower a pen. His invention wrote dots and dashes that stood for letters on a moving strip of paper. Important messages could be flashed in an instant between faraway cities.

These inventions used electric current, but batteries were the only source of electricity. With Oersted's discovery that electricity could produce magnetism, scientists asked the next logical question: Could magnets be used to generate electricity?

Michael Faraday, an English scientist who lived in London, tried to make electricity from magnetism. He built a sensitive meter with a compass needle that showed both the direction and strength of electric flow. He put a strong magnet next to a wire, but the compass needle did not flicker. No electricity flowed.

Faraday did not give up. For more than ten years, he tried different arrangements of the wire. One day in 1831, Faraday thrust a bar magnet into the coil of wire while it was hooked to the electric meter. The needle flicked to one side, showing a small amount of electricity had flowed, but then the needle quickly fell back. Faraday pulled out the bar magnet. The needle flickered again.

Suddenly, Faraday realized the solution. Motion was the key. In Orested's original experiment, moving electrons in a wire upset a compass needle. In the same way, a moving magnetic field puts electrons in motion.

Oersted and Faraday had showed that electricity and magnetism were related. One could produce the other. Rather than electricity and magnetism, there was but one force called electromagnetism.

Making electricity or magnetism from the other is known as electromagnetic induction. One small-scale use of electromagnetic induction is a flashlight that does not need batteries. Instead, a person squeezes a handle that is geared to spin magnets around a coil of wire and send electricity to the flashlight bulb. Another design uses a magnet that slides up and down inside a coil of wire in the handle. This, too, makes electricity by electromagnetic induction.

Michael Faraday's discovery of magnetic induction was important because it proved useful in making practical inventions but also because it revealed the connection between magnetism and electricity.

Michael Faraday had received only the basics of an education from a church Sunday school. England at that time had no free schools, and he was too poor to attend one that charged tuition. To overcome his lack of mathematical training, Faraday invented the visual concept of lines of force rather than equations to describe magnetic and electric fields.

Throughout his life, he continued to test the effect of magnetism upon other quantities. He found connections among what other scientists thought were unrelated subjects. For instance, scientists knew that certain crystals

Everyday Uses of Electromagnets

A short circuit causes too much electricity to flow in a circuit. The wires can overheat and start a fire. A circuit breaker has an electromagnet that remains closed and allows a normal flow of electricity. If a short circuit causes the electric flow to become too great, the increased current causes the electromagnet to pull a switch that turns off the electricity.

Laptops store information using electromagnets.

Digital game machines, portable computers, and some watches use a liquid with crystals that turn the same direction when put in a magnetic field. Magnetic fields control the crystals to display the information on the screens of the electronic devices. Scientists believe it may be practical to publish an entire newspaper on a single sheet of special paper. Rather than turning a page, a person would touch a spot to bring the next page into view.

Computers and other digital devices store information by using electromagnets to write the data. Magnetic fields change the orientation of magnetic domains in the coatings on hard drives.

Because two like magnetic poles repel, it is possible to design vehicles that are held in the air by magnetic repulsion. Magnetic levitation trains float above a track called a guideway. Electromagnets are built into both the train and the guideway. Electromagnets push the train into the air and shove it along the guideway. In 1990, Germany built an experimental maglev train that traveled at a speed of 271 miles (436 km) per hour.

Material that undergoes a type of nuclear reaction known as atomic fusion is heated so hot that it melts anything it touches. Scientists use electromagnets to generate a magnetic field that keeps the hot material away from the walls of its container.

Physicists use a giant ring of electromagnets to accelerate subatomic particles to near the speed of light. The largest one, in Europe, is 16 miles around.

Michael Faraday, an English scientist, worked for more than ten years trying to generate electricity from magnetism.

electricity and magnetism, and magnetism and light.

In addition to his skill as a scientist, he displayed the humility of a sincere Christian. Michael Faraday believed in the Bible as the Word of God and accepted Christ as the guide for his life. He met each week with fellow Christians and served as an elder in his local church congregation. He said, "Religion is concerned with an order of truth different and higher than natural [scientific] truth."

Scientists honor Michael Faraday as one of the greatest scientists of all time. Michael Faraday succeeded because he believed in a simple, unified design in nature, a design put there by the Creator. Light, magnetism, and electricity are not three different subjects but different aspects of the same quantity.

could polarize light. Regular light can vibrate in any direction — left and right, up and down, and any direction in between. Polarized light vibrates in only one direction — up and down, for instance. A second crystal had to be turned a certain way for polarized light to pass through it. Otherwise, the second crystal filtered out the light. Faraday showed that a strong magnetic field would twist the direction of polarized light. Magnetism and light were somehow related.

In chemistry, scientists had found that electricity could pry some metals from their ore. Faraday proved that the amount of freed metal was directly proportional to the amount of electricity.

Faraday succeeded in showing a connection between chemistry and electricity,

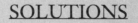

SOLUTIONS

1. A compass points to the north pole of the earth.

2. A moving electric charge produces magnetism.

3. Moving a magnet near a wire causes electricity to flow in the wire.

Light, magnetism, and electricity are related.

T F   1. Unlike static electricity, magnetism was well understood from the time of the Greeks.

T F   2. William Gilbert proved that the compass is drawn toward the North Star.

T F   3. Earth's geographic North Pole and magnetic north pole have the same location.

A B C   4. The force that can attract but not repel is (A. electric charge B. gravity C. magnetism).

T F   5. A negative electric charge can be isolated without a corresponding positive electric charge.

T F   6. Magnets always have a north pole and a south pole.

A B C   7. The metal that a magnet attracts best is (A. aluminum B. gold C. iron).

A B   8. Like magnetic poles (A. attract B. repel) one another.

T F   9. The inverse square law states that a quantity decreases by the square of the distance.

T F   10. Gravity, static electricity, and magnetism all follow the inverse square law.

A B   11. The one that is more difficult to magnetize is (A. soft iron B. steel).

A B   12. When magnetic domains become jumbled, magnetism is (A. lost B. strengthened).

T F   13. An electric current can produce a magnetic field.

A B C D   14. The advantage of an electromagnet is that it (A. can be turned on and off B. does not follow the inverse square law C. can both attract and repel iron D. takes less electricity to operate than a natural magnet).

T F   15. Michael Faraday discovered that a moving magnetic field generates electricity.

A B C D   16. Faraday succeeded in showing a connection between (A. chemistry and electricity B. electricity and magnetism C. magnetism and light D. all of the above).

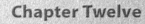

Electromagnetism

Michael Faraday believed that magnetic and electrical forces were related. Some scientists were slow to accept Faraday's discoveries. Faraday had not expressed his ideas with mathematical equations the way Isaac Newton had with his three laws of motion and the law of gravity.

In the 1860s, Faraday realized that he would need to retire, and he began giving away notes about his unfinished experiments to other scientists. One of these scientists was James Clerk Maxwell, a young Scottish physicist, and the best mathematician of the time.

James Clerk Maxwell became the first director of the Cavendish Laboratory in Cambridge, England. His goal was to put Faraday's work on a firm mathematical foundation. First, he began an in-depth study of all that was known about electricity and magnetism. He wrote a book of more than one thousand pages about electromagnetism.

PROBLEMS

1. How do radio waves carry sound?

2. Can light put electrons in motion?

3. Can a spaceship sail on sunlight?

Can You Propose Solutions?

The Cavendish Laboratory in Cambridge, England

Next, he began reducing the information in his book. He simplified the large number of laws that described the properties of electricity and magnetism. Maxwell looked for the original design put in nature by the Creator. He believed that a subject should not confuse and baffle scientists. When it did, he knew they had yet to find the basic laws that described the subject.

Finally, Maxwell developed four equations that became known as Maxwell's field equations. These four equations described all that was known about electricity, magnetism, and — as it turned out — light. The four short equations summarized two hundred years of experimentation and speculation.

Only one person in all of history had written four equations with as much meaning — Isaac Newton. Isaac Newton's three laws of motion and the law of universal gravitation combined force and motion into a series of four related equations. James Clerk Maxwell did the same for electromagnetism. Suppose you wanted to summarize all that is known about force, energy, motion, gravity, electricity, magnetism, and light. You could do it on a postcard by writing down Newton's three laws of motion, the law of gravity, and Maxwell's four electromagnetic field equations.

Maxwell showed that the back and forth motion of an electric charge produces an electromagnetic field. A changing electric current causes a changing magnetic field. But the changing magnetic field then causes a changing electric field. Together, they make electromagnetic waves of the same frequency as the electric field that caused them.

Electromagnetic waves can travel across a vacuum and transfer energy from the source to a distant location.

The electromagnetic waves spread out from their source at a constant speed. From his equations, Maxwell calculated the speed of electromagnetic waves in a vacuum. Their speed was the same as the speed of light. This was strong evidence that light itself was composed of electromagnetic waves.

Maxwell's equations did more than merely summarize what had gone before; with them, scientists could forecast new discoveries. Scientists knew of infrared light and ultraviolet. The electromagnetic spectrum did not stop there.

Electromagnetic wave generator. The hertz, a metric unit for frequency (cycles per second), is named for Rudolf Hertz who built the first device to send and receive electromagnetic radio waves.

Those who understood Maxwell's equations realized they predicted the existence of much longer and much shorter electromagnetic waves.

Rudolf Hertz in Germany read Maxwell's work and studied the equations. He decided he could send and receive electromagnetic waves. After ten years of effort he built an electromagnetic wave generator. Hertz's device consisted of two large metal balls with a small gap of air between them. He connected the metal balls to a circuit with a high voltage electric current. It was an alternating current that flowed first one way and then the other. When he turned the device on, a spark jumped back and forth between the two balls. Across the laboratory, Hertz had a simple coil of wire with a small gap in it. When the larger spark jumped between the large balls, a tiny spark jumped across the gap in the small coil of wire.

In 1889, Hertz announced that his device generated electromagnetic waves a million times longer than waves of visible light. He showed that his waves could be reflected, refracted, and polarized — just like light waves.

The metric unit for frequency, hertz, is named after Rudolf Hertz. A frequency of one hertz is one cycle per second, 1.0 Hz.

Light waves travel through the air in a straight line, but radio waves are longer than light waves. An Italian scientist named Guglielmo Marconi tested how far radio waves could be sent. He found that a layer of air in the upper atmosphere reflected them. In 1901, he communicated across the Atlantic Ocean between England and St. John's, Newfoundland. It was the first invention as a direct result of Maxwell's equations.

Marconi transmitted dots and dashes to spell out messages. At first his invention was called wireless telegraph, but later became known as radio. Scientists found a way for sound waves to pass through a microphone and modulate (or modify) the waves to carry the sound information. Radio transmitters could send speech and music.

The distance up or down on a wave is its amplitude. One way to transmit voice or music is to modulate the amplitude of the waves. An AM radio receives signals of electromagnetic

James Clerk Maxwell

James Clerk Maxwell

James Clerk Maxwell's field equations predicted the existence of radar, radio, television, microwaves, and x rays. The equations not only predicted them, but also described how they would act under different conditions. When electrical engineers design wave-guides in complex electronic equipment such as radio telescopes, they employ the equations to know what to expect. Maxwell's equations are an unfailing guide for the electronics industry.

Many other inventions and discoveries still wait to be found in Maxwell's equations. Companies employ scientists to study the four equations, yet scientists today have only begun to see all of their possibilities.

When asked to name the three greatest physicists of all time, Albert Einstein promptly replied, "Isaac Newton, Michael Faraday, and James Clerk Maxwell." Albert Einstein called Maxwell's achievement "the most profound and most fruitful that physics has experienced since the time of Newton."

Like Michael Faraday, James Clerk Maxwell was also a sincere Christian. He studied the Scriptures, lived a godly life, and held evening prayers and devotions at his home. One of his prayers, says in part, "Almighty God, Who hast created man in Thine own image, and made him a living soul that he might seek after Thee.... that we may believe on Him Whom Thou has sent.... All of which we ask in the name of the same Jesus Christ, our Lord."

Electromagnetic Radiation

Oscillating Fields

All electromagnetic radiation has behavior typical of waves, such as diffraction and interference. It can be thought of as a combination of changing electric and magnetic fields.

Oscillating electric field

Direction of wave's motion is at right angles to the electric and magnetic field

Two fields at right angles

Oscillating magnetic field

Wavelength

Radio Waves

Microwaves

The electromagnetic spectrum. These waves differ from each other in wavelength and frequency and can vary in the amounts of energy they carry.

waves that have had their amplitude modulated. The letters AM stand for amplitude modulation. The AM broadcast band has a frequency between 535,000 hertz (535 kHz) and 1,605,000 hertz (1,605 kHz).

Because AM waves are so long, the signal of an AM radio station can reflect from the ionosphere in the upper atmosphere and be

that have had their frequency modulated. The letters FM stand for frequency modulation. The amplitude is not modified. Instead, the frequency of the radio wave varies slightly to carry the information about the sound.

Because the frequency varies, but not the amplitude (strength) of the signal, every wave of an FM station is sent out at full power. They

Frequency modulation

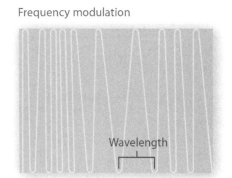

Wavelength

Amplitude modulation

Amplitude

A signal is carried on an electromagnetic wave by modifying the frequency of a wave with constant amplitude(FM), or by modifying amplitude with constant frequency (AM).

received far away, especially at night. However, lightning and other sources of electricity can cause an AM radio station to have static. Electric motors and spark plugs on cars have to be shielded. Otherwise they will interfere with an AM signal.

Another way for radio waves to carry information is to modulate the frequency. The FM radio receives electromagnetic waves

are not as prone to electrical interference. However, the ionosphere does not reflect the shorter waves, so an FM radio signal does not carry as far as an AM signal.

FM stations broadcast signals that can vary as much as 200,000 hertz. The extra space needed to vary the frequency means that FM stations take up more room, called bandwidth, on the radio dial than AM stations. The FM

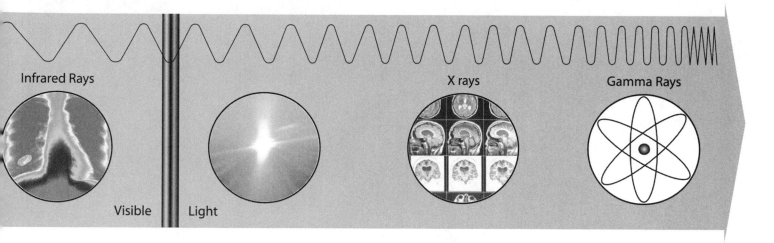

Infrared Rays

Visible Light

X rays

Gamma Rays

broadcast band has a frequency between 88 million hertz (88 MHz) and 108 million hertz (108 MHz). In other words, the AM frequency is measured in kilo (1,000) hertz, but the FM frequency is measured in mega (1,000,000) hertz. Because of the lower frequency, AM radio waves are 1,000 times longer than FM radio waves.

Electromagnetic waves such as radio waves are described as being "below" visible light. A chart of electromagnetic waves usually starts with the longest waves (lowest frequency) at the bottom. An AM radio receives electromagnetic waves of low frequency and long wavelength. The waves become shorter as one goes up the electromagnetic spectrum to FM radio waves. Next are television, microwaves (for both communication and cooking), and then infrared light.

Infrared light waves are longer than red light. A warm object gives off infrared waves. Infrared light can be felt as heat rays. Although human eyes cannot see the heat rays of infrared, some animals can detect the invisible rays of infrared light. The pit viper, a type of snake, has a small pit below the eye that can identify infrared body heat. It leads the snake to its next meal.

Next are the visible light, starting with red as the longest waves, then orange, yellow, green, blue, indigo, and violet as the shortest waves that the human eye can detect. All of the colors — and all other electromagnetic waves — are alike in that they travel at the same speed in a vacuum. They differ in their frequency and wavelength. The human eye can see less than one percent of the entire electromagnetic spectrum.

Electromagnetic waves such as ultraviolet are described as being "above" or "beyond" visible light. Ultraviolet waves are shorter and have a higher frequency. They carry more energy than light waves and are more penetrating than visible light. When exposed to ultraviolet rays, a person's skin develops a tan to protect against those rays.

In 1895, Wilhelm Roentgen, a German physicist, discovered x rays. They were electromagnetic radiation of very short wavelength and extremely high frequency. X rays can penetrate human flesh, but are stopped by bones. Doctors and dentists began using x rays to take pictures of teeth and bones.

Radioactive elements release gamma rays, which have still shorter wavelengths and carry more energy. They can penetrate steel. Gamma rays can expose photograph film in the same way as x rays. Pipelines that carry petroleum cross-country are made of sections of pipe that are welded together. Gamma rays are used to check if there are any defects in joining the sections of pipe. Gamma rays have the highest frequency and shortest wavelength of electromagnetic waves.

The discovery of radio waves and x rays marked the start of ten years (1895–1905) of rapid advancement in physics. Physicists made

Gamma rays are used to check if there are defects in joining the section of pipes on pipelines that carry petroleum cross-country.

so many discoveries, the ten years became known as the second scientific revolution.

Scientific discovery does appear to begin with a new idea or approach followed by a flurry of activity. One key period of change occurred during the time of the ancient Greeks. Pythagoras, Aristotle, Archimedes, and other Greeks relied on observations and logic. They made many important discoveries during the years from 580 to 200 B.C. An even greater step forward began with the introduction of the experimental method during the years from A.D. 1450 to 1650. This period of time is known as the first scientific revolution. The scientific heroes of this period include Copernicus, Galileo, Kepler, Robert Boyle, and others.

The second scientific revolution began in 1895. In the space of ten years, Wilhelm Roentgen discovered x rays, Marconi developed radio, Henri Becquerel revealed the radioactive nature of uranium, Pierre and Marie Curie identified several radioactive elements, Ernest Rutherford explored inside the atom, and Albert Einstein developed the special theory of relativity.

One of Albert Einstein's discoveries concerned the photoelectric effect. Metals such as cesium release electrons when light shines on their surfaces. The first light meters in cameras used this effect. Light struck the surface of the metal and put electrons in motion. The tiny electric current moved a light meter needle that read the brightness of the light. The camera could be adjusted to give the proper exposure.

At first, physicists tried to explain the photoelectric effect in terms of wave motion. Although light waves are small, they are nevertheless far larger than a single electron. A light wave should set many electrons free. Instead, experiments showed that a single electron absorbed the energy of the light wave.

By way of an analogy, think of a water wave rolling in on a sandy beach. Imagine it striking the beach. We expect it to wash over a vast number of sand particles and move each one slightly. Imagine our surprise if the energy of the wave leaves most of the sand particles undisturbed. Instead, the wave shoots at high speed a single grain of sand from the beach.

Experiments with the photoelectric effect found three unexpected results. A dim blue light released a few high-speed electrons. A bright blue light released more electrons but at the same high speed. A dim yellow light released a few low-speed electrons. A bright yellow light released more electrons but at the

Albert Einstein

Albert Einstein

Albert Einstein is recognized as the greatest physicist of the 1900s. He was born in Germany, attended school in Switzerland, and later moved to the United States. He showed no particular promise as a youngster. He was slow to speak. His parents thought he might have a learning disability. He attended school in Switzerland. After graduation, he attended a college that trained him to be a teacher of physics. One of his teachers encouraged him to drop out of school. The teacher said, "You'll never amount to anything, Einstein."

Einstein did graduate, but could not find employment as a teacher. Instead, he worked at a low-paying job as a technical assistant at a patent office. In his spare time, he studied mathematics and physics and read everything he could on science.

In 1905, he published three important research papers. In the first one, Einstein calculated the size of water molecules by how they shoved around tiny pollen grains, an action known as Brownian motion.

His second paper investigated the photoelectric effect. Einstein's theory explained the photoelectric effect with the idea that light had a particle nature.

The third paper was the special theory of relativity. Einstein assumed that the speed of light was constant and that physical laws were identical regardless of the uniform motion of an observer. He concluded that the upper limit to speed was that of light in a vacuum.

He also discovered that, unlike the speed of light, time was not constant. It did depend upon the speed of the observer. This led to the famous twin paradox. Suppose one astronaut stayed on earth, but his twin took off in a ship that accelerated to near the speed of light. After four years aboard the ship, the space-going twin returned to earth. To him, the trip took only four years. He would be only four years older. But his twin left behind on earth would be elderly — 40 or more years would have passed.

Einstein worked out the famous equation, $E = mc^2$, a relationship between energy, E, and mass, m, with c^2, the speed of light squared. The equation explained the vast amount of energy generated by the sun and by nuclear reactions.

He came back to the theory of relativity and developed it more fully as the general theory of relativity. Einstein predicted that the gravity of the sun would bend the path of starlight. Photographs taken during an eclipse in 1919 showed that rays of light from stars had been shifted out of position in the manner he predicted.

Albert Einstein held a strong belief in a Supreme Creator. He said, "My religion consists of humble admiration of the illimitable (limitless) Supreme Spirit who reveals himself in the slight details we are able to perceive with our frail and feeble minds." On another occasion, he was asked where his ideas come from. He said, "Ideas come from God."

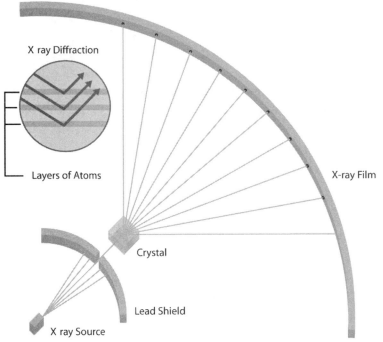

Compton experimented with x rays shot into crystals.

X ray Diffraction

Layers of Atoms

X-ray Film

Crystal

Lead Shield

X ray Source

same low speed. A red light, whether dim or bright, released no electrons at all. No matter how intensely bright the red light, no electrons escaped from the surface of the metal.

The frequency of a light wave is its color — blue light is higher frequency than yellow or red light. The amplitude of a light wave is its brightness. Why did waves of red light, regardless of their brightness, fail to release electrons? Why did blue light, even if it was very dim, release electrons? All attempts to explain the photoelectric effect in terms of wave motion failed.

Albert Einstein explained the photoelectric effect by thinking of light as packets of energy. Later, these bundles of energy became known as photons. A photon was more like a particle than a wave.

According to Einstein, an electron could absorb at most a single photon. Each color had photons of a fixed amount of energy. The amount of energy in a photon of red light was too slight to break an electron free from the metal holding it. Increasing the brightness of red light increased the number of photons but

not their energies. An electron could absorb only one photon at a time, so it was never given enough energy to escape from the surface of the metal.

A photon of yellow light had just enough energy to free an electron. The electron left the surface of the metal at low speed. Turning up the brightness of yellow light produced more photons, but each one still had the same energy. More electrons escaped but they still came away at the same low speed.

A photon of blue light had more than enough energy to free an electron. The electron shot away from the metal at high speed. Each photon freed an electron. So brighter blue light (more photons) increased the number of electrons that were freed. But they all shot away at the same speed.

Albert Einstein went on to develop the theory of relativity. In 1921, he received the Nobel Prize in physics. The honor came not because of his theory of relativity, but because of his explanation of the photoelectric effect.

However, when he first proposed that light had a particle nature, scientists were reluctant to accept the idea. The wave theory of light explained every property of light except the photoelectric effect. Scientists resisted accepting the idea that light had a particle nature based on a single example.

Arthur Holly Compton provided a second example, although it came from an unexpected direction. He experimented with x rays shot into crystals. The regular arrangement of atoms in crystals scattered the x rays. He measured the angle of their scattering. From the data, he hoped to learn about the arrangement of the atoms and electrons in the crystal.

To his surprise, he found the wavelength of the x ray going in did not match the wavelength of the x ray coming out. Imagine shining a beam of blue light at a mirror. You expect the reflected ray to be blue, too. If it reflects as a red ray, you know that something unexpected has taken place. That was exactly what Compton observed. The x rays going into the crystal came out with a different wavelength.

Arthur Holly Compton

Arthur Holly Compton was seven years old when the Wright Brothers made their first flight. He began building model airplanes that flew. While in high school, he designed a full size glider to carry himself as pilot. He built it all himself. He designed the craft, glued together the wooden ribs for wings, and sewed together the fabric to cover them. His family and some professors from Wooster College came to watch the flight. It worked flawlessly.

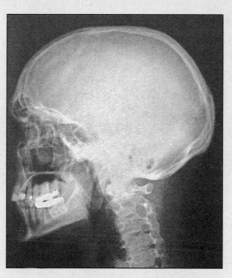

X-ray photograph showing dental work and skull

Arthur Holly Compton began college in 1910 after the major achievements of the years 1895 to 1905 had made their way into college textbooks. When he began his college studies, Arthur Compton thought deeply about what he should do. His family believed in a life of Christian service. His father was a Presbyterian minister.

While attending Wooster College, where his father was dean of the school, young Compton taught Sunday school. He inspired several in his class to become missionaries, but Compton wondered what should be his life work.

His father told him, "There is no calling as high as that of the ministry. However, you have a special interest in the field of science. It is in science that you will do your best work. Your work in this field may become a more valuable Christian service than if you enter the ministry."

After graduation from Wooster, Arthur traveled to Princeton for advanced study. Many of the professors of science were active in various Christian churches. They believed, as he did, that the design of nature offered overwhelming evidence for the existence of an Almighty Designer. He said, "I believe that our universe is not a chaos but an ordered cosmos."

While studying x rays, he invented the term "photon" for a tiny bundle of light energy. In addition to his discoveries with x rays shot into crystals, he also studied cosmic rays. He proved that cosmic rays were extremely powerful subatomic particles that traveled through outer space at nearly the speed of light.

Compton studied the potential of nuclear energy. He agreed that a nuclear chain reaction was possible. He became a lead scientist on the secret Manhattan Project to develop an atomic bomb. His role was to keep scientists focused on the task at hand and working together.

Arthur Compton enjoyed a life of science and Christian service. He said, "From earliest childhood I have learned to see in Jesus the supreme example of one who loves his neighbors and expresses that love in actions that count."

Other scientists confirmed his discovery. They called it the Compton effect. How could he explain the effect he had discovered? What caused the wavelengths of the x rays to lengthen?

Compton knew that when an x ray struck an electron, it changed the velocity of the electron. An electron had mass and velocity. The product of the two was momentum. He knew that momentum was neither gained nor lost during a collision. For the electron to gain momentum, something else had to lose it. Only x rays had struck the electron, but x rays were electromagnetic waves. As a form of energy they had tremendous velocity but no mass. Without mass, they had no momentum. Yet, somehow, they gave momentum to the electron.

He found a simple solution when he treated x rays as particles. The Compton effect could be completely explained if light were particles. A single photon of x ray light struck a single electron. The electron took some of the energy. The x ray decreased in wavelength. Einstein's equation, $E = mc^2$, showed that energy and mass could be interchanged. The loss of energy of an x ray could be treated as a very small change in mass.

Compton's x ray experiments with crystals showed that the photoelectric effect was not the only example of light acting as particles. Scientists now accepted the fact that light was more complex than they had believed.

Was light a wave? Was light a particle? Compton said, "Neither." Light had properties of both. He saw no contradiction in this. In Sunday school classes he taught three aspects of God: God as the ruler of the universe, God as a hero to be admired, and God as a guiding spirit. Could not photons have more than one aspect?

A Scottish physicist named Charles Wilson invented a cloud chamber. When electrons traveled through the chamber, they revealed their path by a series of tiny water droplets that formed in the cloud chamber. The cloud chamber made the Compton effect directly visible. The trail left by electrons in the cloud chamber suddenly changed when x rays struck them.

Scientists now saw other examples that light could exert pressure on material objects. For instance, when a comet passed near the sun, its tail always pointed away from the sun. Sunlight (as well as some solid particles streaming up from the sun) pushed the gases of the comet's tail away from the sun.

Scientists have calculated that sunlight alone can act on large sheets of aluminum foil that are in space. It may be possible to design a solar sailing ship with gigantic aluminum sails that is pushed along by the pressure of sunlight.

In 1927, Arthur Holly Compton won the Nobel Prize for his x ray studies. He shared it with Charles Wilson, the inventor of the cloud chamber.

SOLUTIONS

1. Modify the amplitude or frequency of the radio waves.

2. Electrons are freed when light strikes some metals.

3. Sunlight exerts a slight force on material objects.

Light has both wave and particle attributes.

A B C D   1.   The scientist who developed four equations that summarized electromagnetism was (A. Albert Einstein   B. Isaac Newton   C. James Clerk Maxwell   D. Michael Faraday).

A B C   2.   The speed of electromagnetic waves is (A. greater   B. less   C. the same) as visible light.

A B C D   3.   The first scientist to generate electromagnetic waves was (A. Arthur Compton   B. Guglielmo Marconi   C. Michael Faraday   D. Rudolf Hertz).

T F   4.   FM radio waves carry around the world because they reflect from a layer in the upper atmosphere.

A B   5.   The (A. AM   B. FM) radio band is prone to electrical interference.

A B C D   6.   The M in AM and FM stands for (A. Marconi   B. Maxwell   C. modulation   D. momentum).

           7.   Write the numbers 1 to 4 in the blanks to rank these waves in order from lowest frequency (longest wavelength) to highest frequency (shortest wavelength): _____ blue visible light, _____ AM radio waves, _____ X rays, _____ infrared light.

A B C D   8.   The period 1895–1905 is known as (A. the Aristotle period   B. the atomic age   C. the first scientific revolution   D. the second scientific revolution).

T F   9.   In the photoelectric effect, the speed of electrons emitted depends on the brightness of the light.

T F   10.   Albert Einstein explained the photoelectric effect by thinking of light as particles rather than waves.

A B C D 11.   Albert Einstein won the Nobel Prize in physics because of his research papers about (A. Brownian motion   B. the equation $E = mc^2$ C. photoelectric effect   D. special theory of relativity).

T F   12.   Momentum is the product of mass and color.

T F   13.   Arthur Compton found that an x ray could change the momentum of an electron.

T F   14.   To date, the photoelectric effect is the only example of light acting as particles.

Nuclear Energy

Nuclear energy comes from reactions involving subatomic particles. Although many subatomic particles exist, the three most important ones are the electron, proton, and neutron. They differ in mass, electric charge, and where they are located in an atom. An atom consists of a cloud of electrons surrounding a small, dense nucleus of protons and neutrons.

An electron has a negative electric charge, -1. An electron is the least massive of the three particles. It takes about 1,840 electrons to equal the mass of a proton. An electron is a fundamental particle because it is not made of smaller particles.

A proton has an electric charge that is equal to the charge of an electron but positive rather than negative. A proton is very massive for its size. If a pencil were made entirely of protons without space between them, then it would weigh as much as the

PROBLEMS

1. Can the nucleus of an atom be changed?

2. Is it possible to split an atom?

3. Does anything good come of nuclear reactors?

Can You Propose Solutions?

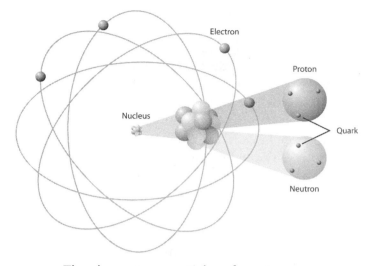

The elementary particles of an atom

Washington Monument. Protons are in the nucleus of an atom.

Protons are made of still smaller particles called quarks. Quarks are believed to be the smallest known building blocks of matter. However, 75 years ago scientists thought protons, neutrons, and electrons were the smallest particles possible. They believed the three elementary particles could not be split into anything smaller, but the proton and neutron are made of quarks, which are smaller.

Physicists have identified six different quarks and given them the names of up, down, top, bottom, strange, and charm. Each quark has a particular mass and charge. Combinations of quarks produce larger particles.

A proton has two up quarks (each with a $+\frac{2}{3}$ charge) and one down quark (with a $-\frac{1}{3}$ charge). The total charge is $2 \times \frac{2}{3} + (-\frac{1}{3}) = +1$.

A neutron has three quarks — one up quark ($+\frac{2}{3}$ charge) and two down quarks (each with $-\frac{1}{3}$ charge). The total charge of a neutron is zero: $+\frac{2}{3} + 2 \times (-\frac{1}{3}) = 0$. Because down quarks are slightly more massive than up quarks, a neutron is slightly more massive than a proton. A neutron is in the nucleus of an atom and helps keep protons from repelling one another.

In its normal state, an atom is electrically neutral. It does carry electric charge, but the number of electrons with a negative charge is equal to the number of protons with positive charge. Overall, it has a neutral charge.

All matter is made of some combination of atoms. Two atoms of the same chemical element always have the same number of protons. Hydrogen, for instance, has one proton. If it had two protons it would not be hydrogen. Instead, it would be helium.

Two atoms of the same chemical element can differ in the number of electrons. If an oxygen atom loses an electron, then it is still oxygen, but it has a positive charge because of the missing electron. If it gains an electron, it is still oxygen, but it has a negative charge because of the extra electron.

Two atoms of the same chemical element can differ in the number of neutrons. Most hydrogen atoms are made of one proton and no neutrons. But some hydrogen atoms have one proton and one neutron. The atom is more massive because of the extra neutron, but it is still a hydrogen atom. It is called an isotope of hydrogen.

Many atoms of the same substance do differ in their mass because of the different number of neutrons. For instance, uranium is the most massive naturally occurring atom. The most common uranium atom, called uranium-238, has 92 electrons, 92 protons, and 146 neutrons. But another type of uranium atom, known as uranium-235, has 92 electrons, 92 protons, but only 143 neutrons.

The number following an atom tells the total number of protons and neutrons. In uranium-238, the 238 equals 92 (number of protons) plus 146 (number of neutrons).

As another example, carbon-14 has six protons and eight neutrons. The number 14 is also known as the atomic mass of the atom. Electrons are ignored because they are so light in weight.

Chemical reactions cannot change the number of protons or neutrons. When hydrogen and oxygen combine to form water, the atoms are electrically attracted to one another. Electrons may switch between atoms or be shared by two atoms, but the nucleus is unchanged.

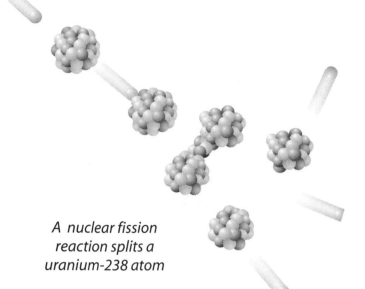

A nuclear fission reaction splits a uranium-238 atom

Nuclear reactions do change the nucleus. The number of protons or neutrons changes. Uranium atoms can undergo radioactive decay and split apart. When the atom breaks apart, it releases energy and one or more small particles. The splitting of an atom into smaller parts is nuclear fission. Fission means to split apart.

Nuclear reactions can also force atoms together. For instance, one type of nuclear reaction involves two hydrogen atoms, each with one proton and one neutron. When they are forced together, the result is a helium nucleus with two protons and two neutrons. The process of forcing together nuclei of atoms is known as nuclear fusion. The word fusion means to melt together.

In the mid-1930s, physicists had learned that nuclear fusion of hydrogen into helium produced the sun's energy. On earth, however, no one knew how to get useful energy from an atom.

It was easier to cause atoms to break apart than to melt them together. In other words, fission appeared to be easier than fusion. Physicists used high-speed particles to slam into atoms and cause them to split, but it took energy to produce the high-speed particles and guide them into the atoms. The amount of energy released by splitting atoms was less than the amount that it took to cause the split. At first, fission produced no useful energy.

Physicists looked for the right particle to slam into a nucleus. Electrons were too lightweight to affect the nucleus. Protons were more massive, but because of their charge, they were repelled by the nucleus. Scoring a direct hit was very unlikely, and the proton was lightweight compared to most nuclei. An alpha particle contained two protons and two neutrons. It was more massive, but it too carried a double positive charge and was repelled by the nucleus.

Enrico Fermi, an Italian scientist, realized that neutrons would work better as atomic bullets. Neutrons were as massive as a proton but carried no charge. They would penetrate deep into the atom.

Most researchers believed faster neutrons would break up a nucleus better than slow neutrons. Fermi discovered this idea to be false. Slow neutrons did better at splitting nuclei than fast ones. Because of their neutral charge, fast neutrons shot clean through a nucleus without being captured. However, slower neutrons were in the neighborhood longer and more likely to be attracted by nuclear forces.

Rather than shattering the nucleus because of their speed, they combined with the nucleus and made it unstable. After a moment, the nucleus came apart.

Fermi sent neutrons through paraffin to slow them. In one of his experiments, he sent slow neutrons into indium. It had 49 protons and 66 neutrons. A slow neutron struck indium and changed it into a tin atom, with 50 protons. Somehow, by gaining a neutron, the indium's proton count went up by one and it became tin. During the reaction, a high-speed electron was emitted. This changed the neutron into a proton.

Uranium with 92 protons was the naturally occurring element with the greatest number of protons. Fermi wondered what would happen if he sent neutrons into uranium nuclei. Would uranium gain a proton as indium did and change into an atom with 93 protons? If so, it would be an entirely new atom that was not found in nature.

He tested the idea. Uranium did become unstable and changed in some way. He believed that neutrons could only cause slight changes in a nucleus, but he could not identify what had happened to the nucleus.

Italy in the 1930s was undergoing turmoil caused by the Italian dictator Benito Mussolini. Enrico Fermi chose to flee from Italy and give up his nuclear researches until he relocated in America.

In the meantime, a woman named Lise Meiter had fled from Germany. A dictator also ruled Germany — Adolph Hitler. Meiter moved to Sweden where she studied the results of Fermi's experiments. She realized that the uranium nucleus had split into two roughly equal pieces. In 1939, Lise Meitner became the first physicist to state that uranium could undergo fission.

When the uranium atom absorbed a neutron, it split into two smaller atoms and released a great amount of energy. In addition, the uranium atom emitted two or three additional neutrons. These secondary neutrons could then cause additional atoms to split, which in turn could cause still more to split. Lise Meiter predicted that a fission reaction could become a self-sustaining chain reaction.

After Enrico Fermi moved to the United States, he became convinced that uranium fission could make a bomb. It would be more powerful than anything imagined. Germany, lead by Adolph Hitler, had invaded Poland in 1939. World War II began. Fermi feared that Hitler would make a nuclear bomb and thus dominate the world.

Fermi and a friend wrote a letter to President Franklin D. Roosevelt. Fermi asked Albert Einstein to sign the letter. Einstein was the best-known scientist in the world. Einstein agreed to send the letter. It said in part, "Some recent work leads me to expect that the element uranium may be turned into a new and important source of energy. It is conceivable — though much less certain — that extremely powerful bombs of a new type may thus be constructed."

President Roosevelt ordered that a bomb be made in secret. The effort was known by the code name of "Manhattan Project." American, British, and Canadian scientists worked on the project. On December 2, 1942, Fermi built the first nuclear reactor. His experiment showed that a chain reaction could be controlled. In July 1945, scientists exploded the first nuclear weapon. The test took place at a remote air force base in New Mexico. Germany had already been defeated, but Japan fought on. After atomic bombs were dropped on two Japanese cities, Japan gave up fighting and World War II ended. The bombs were called A-bombs because their energy came from splitting atoms.

Nuclear fission produces vast quantities of energy compared to the amount of fuel used. Compare nuclear energy to coal. A trainload of coal is about 100 coal cars each holding 100 tons of coal for a total of 10,000 tons of coal. Each day, every day, a large coal-burning electric power station uses a trainload of coal. A nuclear power station can run for a year on 30 tons of uranium or plutonium fuel. A tiny sample of uranium that weighs about the same as a sheet of paper can produce as much energy as 9 tons of coal.

The first nuclear reactions used uranium. The heavy metal is extracted from uranium ore. One ton (2,000 pounds) of uranium ore has only four pounds of uranium. The ore is crushed and treated with an acid to remove uranium. The uranium comes out combined with oxygen. Because of its yellow color, uranium oxide is called yellowcake.

Two types of uranium are mixed together in yellowcake. One type is uranium-238, or U-238, because it has a total of 238 protons and neutrons. The other is called uranium-235, or U-235, because it has a total of 235 protons and neutrons. It is not as plentiful as U-238, but the less plentiful U-235 atoms make the best nuclear fuel.

Separating the two types of uranium is difficult. However, pure U-235 is not required. Instead, the uranium fuel is enriched. Enrichment increases the number of U-235 atoms. First, yellowcake is made into a gas.

Nuclear power plant showing the cooling towers

The gas is run through a long pipe. One atom out of every 100 is a U-235 atom at the start. Lighter U-235 atoms speed down the pipe faster than heavier U-238 atoms. The gas caught at the end has more U-235 atoms. Five atoms out of every 100 are U-235 atoms at the end.

Uranium fuel is pressed into small, solid pellets. At the power station, about 30 tons of uranium pellets are loaded into long fuel rods. The fuel rods are lowered into the reactor.

Something interesting happens to the U-238 atoms that are mixed with U-235. When a U-235 atom breaks down, or decays, it splits into two smaller atoms. At the same time, it releases energy and three neutrons. When neutrons strike the heavier U-238 atoms a nuclear transformation occurs. Rather than splitting, the nucleus gains two protons but loses a neutron. It becomes an entirely different substance named plutonium. Plutonium is named after the planet Pluto, just as uranium is named after the planet Uranus.

Plutonium-239 has 94 protons and 145 neutrons. Plutonium is not a naturally occurring element. Instead, it is made from uranium in a nuclear reactor. Pure plutonium is a silver-colored metal. Plutonium is warm because its atoms constantly break down and release heat.

Plutonium is a nuclear fuel, too, but it must be separated from the spent uranium fuel before it can be used. Many countries reprocess nuclear fuel for plutonium, but it is a dangerous and costly task. The United States does not reprocess fuel.

A breeder reactor is a special reactor that actually produces more fuel than it uses. It has an inner core made of uranium-235 and plutonium. A ring of rods filled with uranium-238 surrounds the inner core. The outer ring of uranium-238 captures neutrons that escape from the core. The uranium is changed into plutonium. France, Japan, and Germany use fast reactors to make plutonium fuel.

A chain reaction can die out. Neutrons from fission travel at 60,000 miles (96,600 km) per second. They can zip out of the fuel before they cause other atoms to split. They need to be slowed to about 1,400 miles (2,250 km) per second. A moderator slows neutrons. The moderator runs between the fuel rods. Neutrons enter the moderator and bounce around. They lose some of their speed. Most reactors today use water as a moderator. Sometimes graphite, a form of pure carbon, is used. Moderators of water or graphite keep a chain reaction going.

Care must be taken so that a chain reaction does not get out of hand. Control rods keep the nuclear reaction going at the right speed.

Metals such as cadmium or boron make the rods. These metals absorb neutrons. Control rods are pulled out to speed up the reaction. Control rods are pushed in to slow it down. Pushing them all the way in shuts off the nuclear reaction.

Uranium or plutonium fuel produces heat inside the core of the reactor. The most important rule about running a nuclear reactor is that the fuel rods must not overheat. Otherwise they would melt and cause the reactor to explode.

Coolant carries away heat and cools fuel rods. Ordinary water is used as a coolant in most reactors in the United States. Water is pumped around the fuel rods. The water flows through a heat exchanger. Coolant water gives up its heat to water that is in a separate set of pipes. Water from the reactor core never mixes with outside water. The coolant goes back to the reactor. The outside water changes to steam that spins a turbine to generate electricity.

After passing through the turbine, the water still carries a lot of heat. To drain it into a river or lake would cause heat pollution. It might kill fish or cause other problems. Most nuclear power plants condense the steam back into liquid water. The water is cooled in a tower that stands next to most nuclear power stations. Great clouds of moisture rise from the towers.

Today, almost 450 nuclear power stations have been built around the world. They generate electricity for use in homes, businesses, and factories. About 12 percent of the world's electrical energy comes from nuclear fission. Nuclear reactors produce 10 percent of the electricity used in Canada. Nuclear reactors supply about 20 percent of the electricity for the United States. Some countries get most of their electrical energy from nuclear power. More than three-fourths of France's energy comes from nuclear power.

In the United States and some other countries, the reliance on nuclear energy has declined. In 1990, the United States had 111 nuclear reactors. Some were old and had to be shut down. By 2002, the United States had 104 operating reactors. The last United States reactor was built in 1996. Sweden and Germany decided to stop using nuclear power all together. Why?

One reason is cost. A nuclear power station can cost five billion dollars. Power stations that burn fossil fuels (petroleum or coal) can be built more quickly and at less cost. A nuclear power station has a useful lifetime of about 35 years. During those years, it must make enough electricity to earn a profit. Power companies are not certain that nuclear power stations will pay for themselves.

Another reason is public opinion. Some people object to having nuclear power stations near their homes. They fear nuclear accidents. Most people think of atomic bombs when they think of nuclear reactions. The first use of the fission reaction was as a weapon that ended World War II.

Shortly after World War II, powerful fusion bombs were built. They were many times more powerful than A-bombs. They were called H-bombs. The H stood for hydrogen, because hydrogen is the chief ingredient in a fusion bomb. In fusion, two lighter atoms combine to form a heavier one. Fusion of hydrogen

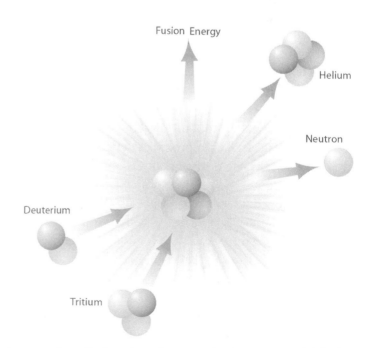

In a nuclear fusion reaction two hydrogen nuclei (tritium and deuterium) fuse to form one helium nucleus

produces five times more energy than the fission of the same weight of uranium, but forcing protons and neutrons together to make a fusion reaction requires intense pressure and high temperatures. The sun gets its energy by fusion. The core of the sun has the high temperatures and great pressure required for the reaction to take place. On earth, only a fission reaction (using uranium or plutonium) produces enough heat and pressure to start a fusion reaction to combine hydrogen to give helium.

Nuclear fusion has a big advantage over fission. It does not produce radioactive wastes, but no one has yet figured out how to use a fusion reaction to generate electricity in a way that is practical. Fusion has only been used to make bombs.

Physicists believe it may be possible to coach hydrogen atoms into producing nuclear fusion without intense temperatures and pressure. The process is called cold fusion. However, no one has yet succeeded in producing energy by cold fusion. It is one of the great, unsolved problems of science.

How does splitting a nucleus — fission — or combining two nuclei — fusion — produce energy? In either case, the total mass after the reaction is less than the total mass before the reaction. When the mass of all the particles involved are totaled, some mass has disappeared. The loss of mass is changed into an equivalent amount of energy as given by Einstein's mass energy equation: $E = mc^2$, with E the energy, m the mass, and c^2 the speed of light squared.

For instance, after it splits apart, the total mass of all the pieces of a uranium nucleus is less than that of the original uranium nucleus. The missing mass is slight, only about $1/10$ of one percent (that is, 0.001) of the mass of the nucleus.

The energy can be heat, light, or the kinetic energy carried away by high-speed particles. In the original uranium nucleus, the extra energy held the atom together. The energy itself gave the nucleus more mass. The fact that energy can show itself as mass is one of the consequences of Einstein's mass energy equation.

Nuclear reactions are so powerful because the speed of light is squared. The speed of light is a large number. The quantity c^2 makes it even more enormous. A little bit of matter goes a long way toward making a lot of energy.

SOLUTIONS

1. Nuclear reactions change the number of protons or neutrons in the nucleus.

2. Neutrons cause an atom's nucleus to come apart.

3. Nuclear fission generates about 12 percent of the world's electrical energy.

A small amount of matter can make a lot of energy.

A B C D 1. The one that is not made of smaller particles is a (A. electron B. hydrogen atom   C. neutron   D. proton).

A B C 2. The more massive subatomic particle is the (A. electron B. neutron   C. proton).

A B C 3. A hydrogen atom changes to a helium atom if it gains (A. a neutron B. a proton   C. an electron).

A B 4. The splitting of an atom into smaller parts is nuclear (A. fission B. fusion).

T F 5. It is easier to cause the nuclei of atoms to break apart than to melt them together.

A B C D 6. Enrico Fermi discovered that the best particles to cause the break-up of a nucleus were (A. electrons   B. helium nuclei C. neutrons   D. protons).

A B C D 7. The first person to state that uranium could undergo fission and produce a self-sustaining chain reaction was (A. Albert Einstein B. Enrico Fermi   C. Franklin D. Roosevelt   D. Lise Meiter).

T F 8. A breeder reactor changes uranium-238 into plutonium.

A B C D 9. The purpose of a moderator is to (A. absorb neutrons   B. cool the reactor   C. generate heat   D. slow neutrons).

A B 10. The total mass after a nuclear reaction is (A. less   B. more) than the total mass before the reaction.

T F 11. More than half of the electricity used in the United States comes from nuclear reactors.

T F 12. The first cold fusion reactor was built in 2002.

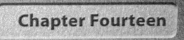
Future Physics

In the early years of the 20th century, it became clear that the laws of physics could not describe the behavior of extremely small objects, such as atoms and subatomic particles. The accepted laws worked especially well when applied to large objects such as baseballs and moving cars, but as scientists studied light and smaller particles, they came to the conclusion that their laws simply did not tell the whole story.

Years before the second scientific revolution, scientists had been unable to explain something that they called the ultraviolet catastrophe. Their calculations showed that any hot object, such as a fireplace, should emit so much ultraviolet light as to burn anyone incautious enough to warm himself or herself by the fire. Yet, people did warm themselves by a fire without being burned to a crisp. The catastrophe was that light did not follow the equations they used every day.

PROBLEMS

1. Which color gives off heat better?

2. Can we measure all of the properties of an object?

3. Is anything left to discover in physics?

Can You Propose Solutions?

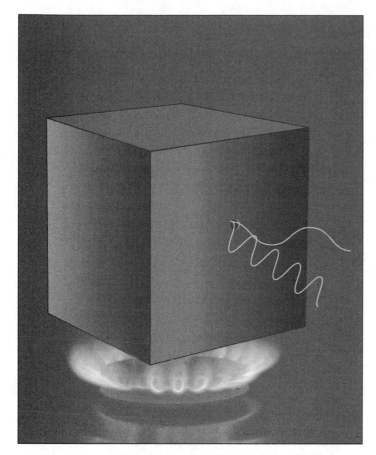

Scientists predicted that when a blackened box was heated the ultraviolet light would carry away more energy than visible light. However the amount of ultraviolet light was much less than predicted.

Everyone knows that a black object will absorb light energy and grow warmer better than a silver colored object. What may not be as well known is that when a black object is heated, it radiates heat better than a silvery object. In fact, a black object radiates heat better than one of any other color. Although it grows warmer in sunlight quicker than other colors, it also cools faster at night than other colors.

Scientists did experiments with black objects. Usually, they built a container with blackened inner walls and a tiny hole in it. They measured the wavelength of light that came out of the hole as they heated the box. The light could be divided into two categories. One was electromagnetic waves of low frequency and long wavelengths such as infrared light. The other was electromagnetic waves of high frequency and short wavelength such as ultraviolet light. According to what was known about electromagnetic waves and black box radiation, scientists predicted that ultraviolet light would carry away more energy from the black box than visible light.

Their predictions failed. The amount of ultraviolet light was far less than predicted.

In 1900, Max Planck, a German physicist, examined the equations to see why the black box did not emit light as predicted. The equations had been developed with the assumption that light was continuous. Light energy could always be of any size. No matter how small, a still smaller sample of light energy could exist.

Max Planck developed new equations to predict the spread of energy coming out of a heated black box. His new equations correctly described the experimental data. The equations are still used today.

Max Planck's equations did not allow light to be continuous. At some point, he arrived at a smallest piece of light. Electromagnetic energy could only be emitted in exact multiples of a tiny bundle of energy that he called a quantum. (The plural of quantum is quanta.) According to Planck's equations, the magnitude of a quantum of light was proportional to the frequency of the light (color).

To change the proportion into an equation, he used the letter "h" to stand for the proportionality constant. Recall, we cannot say that inches equal feet. Instead, we multiply feet by 12 to get inches. The 12 is the proportionality constant. In the same way, Planck could not write E = frequency, but instead he wrote E = h × frequency, with h being the proportionality constant. The constant is an extremely small number. It has since become known as Planck's constant.

Let's look at Planck's equation E = h × f with E the energy, h Plank's constant, and f the frequency of light. As frequency increases, so does the energy. As frequency decreases, the energy becomes less, too. Infrared light has a lower frequency than ultraviolet light. A single quantum of infrared light does not have as much energy as a single quantum of ultraviolet light. As the frequency increases, it becomes

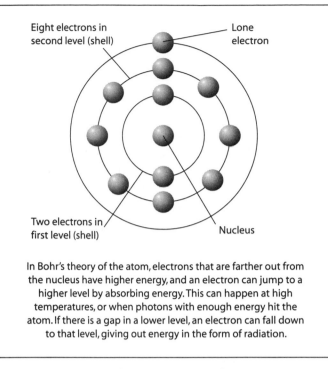

Eight electrons in
second level (shell)

Lone
electron

Two electrons in
first level (shell)

Nucleus

In Bohr's theory of the atom, electrons that are farther out from
the nucleus have higher energy, and an electron can jump to a
higher level by absorbing energy. This can happen at high
temperatures, or when photons with enough energy hit the
atom. If there is a gap in a lower level, an electron can fall down
to that level, giving out energy in the form of radiation.

Diagram of Bohr's model of the atom

more and more difficult to collect enough energy to make the higher frequency quanta. The black box radiates infrared light quanta easier than ultraviolet light quanta.

Planck's use of light quanta explained why the black box did not radiate as much ultraviolet light as the older equations predicted. However, scientists were slow to accept the idea of particles of energy. In fact, Max Planck was not entirely convinced, but in 1905, Einstein used the concept of quanta of light to explain the photoelectric effect.

By 1918, it became clear that Max Planck's idea of energy quanta was real. He received the Nobel Prize for his discovery. Planck's constant, h, has become as important in physics as pi, π, in mathematics.

Planck's discovery of quanta also helped scientists understand the orbit of electrons around the nucleus of atoms. Electrons did not appear to follow the same rules as larger objects such as planets or satellites. When an object in orbit loses energy, it spirals closer to the body it is orbiting. Imagine what happens to a satellite in low earth orbit. Its path slowly decays as it loses energy due to the slight friction with the upper reaches of the earth's atmosphere. Each orbit is slightly lower than

the previous one. If something were not done, it would burn up as it reached the thicker part of earth's atmosphere. Booster rockets can be fired, and the satellite will spiral into a higher orbit.

Electrons, however, did not spiral closer to the nucleus as they lost energy; instead, they jumped to a much smaller orbit. Electrons did not slowly increase their distance when they gained energy; instead, they jumped to a higher orbit.

The energy to send them to a higher orbit had to be just right. If they got less than the right amount, rather than going up part way, they stayed where they were. Their orbit did not change.

In 1913, the Danish physicist Niels Bohr took up the problem of electron orbits. He based his work on observations of the hydrogen atom. Hydrogen is the simplest atom with only one proton, one electron, and no neutrons. The electron could be in different orbits depending on its energy. The closest one was known as the ground state. To move into a higher orbit the electron had to gain energy, but not just any amount of energy would do. Each orbit required a certain amount of energy, and if the electron did not receive that energy, it stayed in place.

Bohr found that electromagnetic waves were absorbed or released only by electrons as they moved higher or lower. An atom radiated energy only if an electron fell from a higher orbit to a lower one. An atom absorbed energy only if an electron jumped from a lower orbit into a higher one, but the amount released or absorbed was by very specific amounts. Each electron could have a series of orbits, but each orbit had a certain fixed distance from the nucleus and a certain fixed amount of energy.

In describing the orbits, Bohr found two constants at work. One was Planck's constant, h, and the other was 2π. Niels Bohr's work on describing the possible orbits of electrons once again showed that energy comes in discrete packets or quanta.

However, one question still needed to be answered. Maxwell's electromagnetic field equations showed that an electric charge undergoing acceleration must radiate energy. Acceleration is a change in speed or a change in direction. An electron carried an electric charge. As it orbited the nucleus, an electron constantly changed direction. So in whirling around a nucleus, an electron should radiate energy and fall closer to the nucleus, but that did not occur. Instead, the electron stayed in a carefully defined orbit. An electron did emit or absorb energy when it jumped from one orbit to another, but as long as it stayed in any one orbit, it emitted no electromagnetic radiation despite undergoing constant acceleration (change in direction). Scientists simply had no explanation for this observation.

One step in the direction to a solution came from Prince Louis de Borglie, a French physicist. He'd come from a noble family, so "Prince" was a title, not his name. At first, he had not been interested in science. During World War I, he offered his service to France and became a radio operator. The tallest structure at that time was the Eiffel Tower in Paris, and it made a good radio antenna. The Eiffel Tower was where his role as a radio officer kept him.

After the war, he studied quantum physics. It had been proven by then that light had a particle nature. De Borglie wondered if matter could have a wave nature. His investigation convinced him that matter could have a wave nature. He then wondered about the size of the

The Eiffel Tower in Paris, because it was the tallest structure in France, made a good radio antenna during World War I.

wave. Would it be large enough to detect, or would a matter wave be far too small to be seen by any known way of looking at matter?

He used two equations, $E = mc^2$, $E = h \times f$, and the fact that the speed of a wave is equal to the frequency times the wavelength, to calculate the wavelength of matter. The calculations were not particularly difficult. They had not been done simply because no one had thought to do them. De Borglie found that the wavelength of a particle was equal to Planck's constant divided by the momentum of the particle.

His calculations showed that matter waves were very short indeed. For an object the size of a baseball, or even an atom, they were far too small to be detected, but the electron was a different story. Its matter wave was about the same size as one for x rays. (They are not the same type of wave. An x ray is electromagnetic; a matter wave is not electromagnetic.)

De Borglie believed the wave of an electron would be long enough to be detected. Electrons should produce interference patterns similar to ones made when light waves or water waves interfere with one another.

For instance, suppose you stood over a small pond and dropped two stones into the pond about one foot apart. Each stone would cause circular waves that radiate outward. When the waves crossed paths, they would sometimes meet crest-to-crest or trough-to-trough and make a big

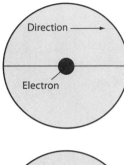

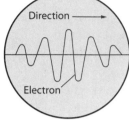

Electron as a particle and as a wave

disturbance on the surface of the water. In other places, the waves would meet crest to trough and leave the surface of the water undisturbed. This pattern of high points, low points, and undisturbed water is an interference pattern.

The wave nature of light produces interference patterns, too. Thomas Young, an English scientist, was the first person to show the interference of light. He began with pure light of a single color and sent it through a hole in a screen. The hole acted as a source of light. The waves spread out from the opening as if it were a source of light.

A short distance away, Thomas Young set another screen with two holes separated from each other. The light waves passed through the holes and radiated outward to land on the third and final screen. On the final screen, where the

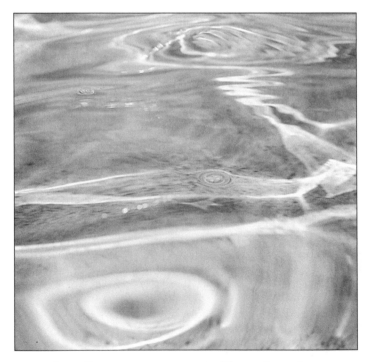

Interference waves created from dropping two stones into a pond

waves reinforced one another, Thomas Young saw a bright band. Where they interfered with one another was a dark spot. The interference pattern of light is very similar to the ripples from two stones dropped into a pond.

To test electrons for their wave nature, man-made holes could not be made small enough. Instead, scientists used metallic crystals. In the modern version of the experiment, a narrow beam of electrons is sent through a thin film of titanium-nickel alloy. The atoms of the alloy have a regular structure. The structure separates the electron beam into several beams that spread outward. The beams then interfere with one another. In places, they cancel each other out. In other places, they reinforce one another. The electrons produce an interference pattern that is typical of waves. Electrons have a wave nature.

The fact that electrons have a wave nature made it possible to explain why electrons could have a limited number of orbits of a particular size around the nucleus. Think of a guitar string and a wave that it can make. For any string of a particular length, mass, and tension, it has a fundamental frequency at which it vibrates. The wave has to fit on the string. In the same way, an electron's wave has a fundamental frequency. It has to fit around its orbit. When it is in the ground state, an electron is at its lowest orbit, and its wave is at its fundamental frequency.

When you hold a guitar string in the middle and pick the string, it will vibrate in two parts. It vibrates at its first overtone. In the same way, when an electron gains energy, it can move to a new orbit, but the new orbit must be some multiple of its fundamental frequency.

When an electron wave exactly fills its orbit, it is a standing wave. The electron no longer has the motion that would require it to radiate energy according to Maxwell's equations. The wave nature of an electron not only explains its orbits at certain distances from the nucleus, but also explains how it avoids radiating energy as it stays in that orbit.

If a string is plucked at its center, it will vibrate with one loop, as in figure a, giving off the lowest pitched tone. By temporarily touching the string at its middle and plucking it at either of the quarter points it can be set into vibration in two loops, figure b. It then has exactly twice the frequency.

Some people find it difficult to understand how one experiment will show that an electron has a wave nature but another experiment will show that an electron has a particle nature.

Whether an object behaves as a particle or a wave depends on your choice of apparatus for looking at it. We use different instruments to measure different things. For instance, we use a thermometer to measure temperature, but we uses a balance scale to measure mass. If we relied only on the thermometer to find facts about a substance, we would say it has a particular temperature, but we could not detect any mass. If we used the balance scale, we would find the object has mass, but could detect no temperature. Yet, it has both mass and temperature.

In the same way, experiments can only reveal one particular property of an electron but not another. Some experiments reveal only facts about the particle nature of the electron.

Other experiments reveal facts about the wave nature of an electron. The properties that we observe about an electron depend on the experiment that we devise to study the electron. Each one can tell us something about the electron, but neither can tell us everything about the electron.

In fact, quantum physics revealed that scientists are limited in how much we can learn about an electron or any other particle at any one instant in time. This disagreed with the commonly held view during the 1800s that science could find all the properties about an object such as its mass and velocity.

Simon Laplace lived in the late 1700s and early 1800s. He was a French astronomer and mathematician who stated that the entire history of the universe from beginning to end could be calculated if the position and velocity of every particle in it were known for any one instant of time. Most scientists agreed with this view, although they knew that the actual task of doing the calculation would be impossible.

But even if the problem of the immense calculation was overcome, Laplace's idea is impossible. Werner Heisenberg proved that the precise position, mass, and velocity could not be known for any particle, much less all the particles in the universe. His discovery is known as the Heisenberg uncertainty principle.

Werner Heisenberg was born in 1901 in Germany. He grew up as many exciting changes took place in the world of physics. Werner traveled in Copenhagen, Denmark, to serve as an assistant to Niels Bohr, the great Danish scientist. Bohr, like most other physicists, built a mental image of how an atom looked. He then developed

Simon Laplace

The blurred motion of a cyclist can be used to calculate the speed of the bicycle, but its specific location at any one instant of time cannot be known.

mathematical equations to explain the workings of their model. He modified the model and the mathematical equations to match new information.

Werner Heisenberg believed one should work from the observations alone. He did not try to build an imaginary picture of the inside of an atom. He developed a new form of mathematics known as quantum mechanics.

Nuclear scientists tried to measure the position, mass, and speed of subatomic particles. Speed and mass combined is known as momentum. Heisenberg became convinced no one could measure position and momentum perfectly. A more accurate measurement of one quantity causes the other one to be less precisely known. The equations of quantum physics told him it was impossible to know both accurately at the same instant.

Here's a simple example. Suppose you want to measure the speed of a friend on a bicycle. You set a camera beside the bicycle path to take a picture of the bicycle as it goes by. The camera has its shutter speed set at ¼ of a second. The picture will show the bicycle as a blur. The blur shows how far the bicycle traveled in

¼ of a second. Knowing the distance and time, you can calculate its speed.

You cannot tell the exact position of the bicycle because its motion blurs the image. You reset the camera to take the picture more quickly. A fast shutter speed gives a sharp image of the bicycle. You can see its exact location when you took the photograph. But you can no longer figure the speed. Without the blur, you don't know how far it traveled while the shutter was open.

In 1927, Werner announced the Heisenberg uncertainty principle. A skilled scientist with perfect equipment cannot capture everything about a system under study. Heisenberg's uncertainty principle shows that science cannot know everything. Some matters are beyond the tools of scientists to grasp.

The uncertainty principle withstood many tests. In 1930 the Nobel Prize committee recognized his discovery of this principle. They awarded Werner Heisenberg the Nobel Prize in Physics.

It is difficult to identify the main ideas of physics in the last 100 years, but most people would list Planck's explanation of black body radiation, Einstein's explanation of the photoelectric effect, Einstein's theory of relativity, Bohr's model of the atom, De Borglie's proposal of matter waves, and Heisenberg's uncertainty principle.

The laws of quantum physics governed how subatomic particles interacted with one another. There is a difference between a scientific discovery and the application of the discovery. For instance, James Clerk Maxwell discovered that a whole range of electromagnetic waves existed. Hertz and Marconi took this scientific discovery and invented radio. The theory of quantum physics was used to guide inventors to a large number of modern inventions, too.

Imagine ordinary citizens of 1895 trying to guess what the next 100 years might bring. Could they imagine such things as seeing beneath human skin (x-ray photographs) or wireless telegraphs (radio)? Would they imagine a form of energy so powerful that it could destroy a large city (nuclear weapons) or machines that soared higher than the highest mountains (airplanes and rockets)? Could they imagine beams of light so powerful as to cut through steel (lasers), or personal communication devices that one could carry in a pocket (cell phones)? Could they imagine communication satellites or Global Positioning Systems (GPS)?

The Internet, computers, artificial satellites, microwaves, transistors, integrated circuits, light-emitting diodes, magnetic resonance imaging, electron microscopes, space probes beyond the solar system — all of these inventions came after the discoveries of the second scientific revolution.

What can be proposed now that might take place in the next 20 years? If you become a physicist, what problems can you attack that still need to be solved? Here is a short list.

Cold fusion. Fusion combines lighter weight atoms into heavier ones. Fusion does not produce as much harmful radiation as fission, and generates about five times as much energy. Today, the usual way to start a fusion reaction is with extremely high temperatures and pressure. The first fusion reaction required the blast of an atomic bomb to get it going. If a nuclear fusion reaction could be done on the small scale at ordinary temperatures it would forever change the world. Energy would become plentiful and cheap.

Broadcast energy. The United States is crisscrossed with high voltage power lines. Homes and factories are wired to carry the energy where it is needed. Ice storms, floods, and other natural disasters sweep away power lines and plunge cities into darkness. Small amounts of energy are carried by the electromagnetic waves used by radio and cell phones. Could the amount be increased so wires connecting electrical devices could be eliminated — and do so without danger to human health? Broadcast energy would make it possible for spaceships to leave earth without carrying the heavy fuel that they need for long voyages.

Faster-than-light communication.
The speed of light is the upper limit as far as physicists have been able to determine. Communication between distant points takes longer because of this cosmic speed limit. Perhaps you have noticed that in live news broadcasts a reporter in a distant country seems to pause before answering the news anchor's question. The signal carrying the anchor's question must travel up to a communication satellite, then the signal is flashed around the world to another satellite, and back down to the ground and the reporter. The reporter's answer must make the return trip. The travel time becomes noticeable because of the limitation of the speed of electromagnetic waves. When the distances are

Communication satellites are made possible by quantum mechanics.

Is it possible that someday students will be able to utilize a matter wave transmitter to get their lunches?

Nanotechnology. Nano means extremely small. Machines no bigger than large molecules are examples of nanotechnology. Some scientists envision such machines being capable of working individually but coming together to make a larger machine. In medicine, nano devices could be injected into the body and flow throughout the bloodstream. They could be programmed to look for defects or other harmful conditions. Once the problem is located, several of them could link together to transmit a photograph of the problem to a sensor outside the body. Or the nano devices could link together to build a larger machine capable of repairing the defect.

Cryogenic. Low temperature research also holds promise of changing the world. Several substances become extremely good conductors of electricity when their temperatures are lowered to near absolute zero. Superconductors may make possible high-speed vehicles that float on magnetic fields and cross-country communication lines with zero resistance to electric flow.

even greater, such as from the earth to a space probe on Mars, several minutes elapse as one communicates with the other. Can the delay be shortened? Will physicists discover a way to communicate faster than light?

Matter transmission and replication. Can a matter wave transmitter be built to beam matter from one place to another? To replicate means to copy. Will future discoveries make it possible to replicate food without growing it? Could a person dial in numbers on a plate-sized container, remove the top, and inside have a meal that is ready to eat?

Control of gravity. Gravity only attracts. Electrostatic forces and magnetic forces both attract and repel. Can a way be found to make gravity repel? Would it be possible to build a gravity shield so that the effects of gravity are weakened? According to Newton's law of gravity, the strength of gravitational attraction depends on distance — the greater the distance, the weaker the force. Can space be distorted so two nearby objects affect one another as if they are farther apart? It is known that an intense gravity field can bend light. Would the reverse be possible — use of electromagnetism to affect gravity? Control of gravity would propel ships without rockets. On a personal level, many people have limited strength in their arms and legs. They are mobile by wheelchairs. Control of gravity would make it possible to walk, even on weak legs.

SOLUTIONS

1. Black surfaces radiate heat better than light colored ones.

2. The speed, mass, and location of an object cannot all be known precisely.

3. Many problems are unsolved in physics.

Matter has both particle and wave attributes.

? Questions

A B   1. In the black box experiment, the amount of ultraviolet light was (A. far less B. many times greater) than predicted.

T F   2. Max Planck found that the smallest quantum of light was proportional to its speed.

A B   3. An ultraviolet quantum has (A. more   B. less) energy than an infrared quantum.

T F   4. Electrons change orbits only by absorbing or emitting set amounts of energy.

A B   5. The one with a wave long enough to be detected is (A. an electron B. a baseball).

T F   6. Light waves can interfere with one another.

A B   7. The ground state, or lowest orbit of an electron, corresponds to its (A. fundamental frequency   B. highest overtone).

A B C D   8. The first particle shown to have a wave nature was (A. an alpha particle B. an electron   C. a gamma ray   D. a proton).

T F   9. The properties that we observe about an electron depend on the experiment that we devise to study the electron.

10. The Heisenberg uncertainty principle states that the precise position, mass, and _____ for any particle cannot be determined exactly.

Matching

11. _____ Niels Bohr
12. _____ Louis de Borglie
13. _____ Max Planck
14. _____ Werner Heisenberg

a. Developed a model of the atom and electron orbits
b. Explained black body radiation by using energy quanta
c. Developed the uncertainty principle
d. Proposed matter waves and calculated their wavelengths

Bibliography

FOR FURTHER READING — AGE APPROPRIATE

Berger, Melvin. *Our Atomic World*. New York: Franklin Watts, 1989.

Challoner, Jack. *Energy*. New York: Dorling Kindersley, 1993.

Cole, Joanna. *The Magic School Bus and the Electric Field Trip*. New York: Scholastic Press, 1997.

Graham, Ian. *Nuclear Power*. Austin, TX: Raintree Steck-Vaughn, 1999.

Lauw, Darlene. *Science Alive! Electricity*. New York: Crabtree Publishing, 2002.

Morris, Henry M. *Men of Science, Men of God*. Green Forest, AR: Master Books, 1982.

Rinard, Judith E. *Book of Flight*. Buffalo, NY: Firefly Books, Inc., 2001.

Robinson, Fay. *Solid, Liquid, or Gas?* Chicago, IL: Childrens Press, Inc., 1995.

Seller, Mick. *Wheels, Pulleys and Levers*. New York: Shooting Star Press, 1995.

Snedden, Robert. *Nuclear Energy*. Chicago, IL: Reed Educational & Professional Publishing, 2002.

Taylor, Barbara. *Force and Movement*. New York: Franklin Watts, 1990.

REFERENCE FOR OLDER READERS

Glazebrook, R.T. *James Clerk Maxwell and Modern Physics*. New York: MacMillan & Co., 1896.

Gribbin, John. *In Search of Schrödinger's Cat*. New York: Bantam Books, 1984.

Hart, Michael H. *The 100: A Ranking of the Most Influential Persons in History*. Secaucus, NJ: Carol Publishing Group, 1993.

Livingston, James D. *Driving Force*. Cambridge, MA: Harvard University Press, 1996.

McEvoy, J.P., and Oscar Zarate, *Introducing Quantum Theory*. Thriplow, Royston, UK: Icon Books Ltd., 2004

McKenzie, A.E.E. *The Major Achievements of Science*. New York: Simon and Schuster, 1960.

Yenne, Bill. *100 Inventions that Shaped World History*. San Mateo, CA: Bluewoods Books, 1993.

INTERNET RESOURCES.

Caution to parents: The contents of these sites were confirmed at the time of publication. However, Internet sites can change and become inappropriate. Check these sites before they are used.

www.eia.doe.gov/kids/ Energy Kid's Page at the United States Department of Energy.

www.nyu.edu/pages/mathmol/textbook/statesofmatter.html States of Matter web page at New York University.

www.eia.doe.gov/fuelnuclear.html United States Department of Energy tells about nuclear reactors and uranium enrichment.

http://nobelprize.org/search/all_laureates_yd.html All about Nobel Prize winners.

www.greatachievements.org/ National Academy of Engineering lists the greatest achievements during the 1900s.

www.noao.edu/kpno/ Kitt Peak National Observatory has some of the nation's largest telescopes.

Answers to Chapter Questions

Chapter 1
1. C – matter
2. F – They seldom did experiments.
3. T 4. F – length and weight
5. C – a vacuum 6. time
7. D – rolled them down a ramp
8. D – change in speed
9. A – 32 ft/sec^2
10. 53 miles per day. Average speed is the distance divided by the time: speed = distance/time = 3,710 miles/ 70 days = 53 mi/da.
11. 7.5 mi/hr × sec. Acceleration = (change in speed)/(change in time) = (60 mi/hr) (8 sec) = 7.5 mi/hr × sec.
12. 31.8 ft/sec. v_f = a × t = (5.3 ft/sec^2) (6 sec) = 31.8 ft/sec

Chapter 2
1. F – velocity includes direction as well as speed 2. T
3. F – force must act on a moving object to slow it to a stop
4. A – friction 5. B – Galileo
6. D – velocity
7. F – every object has inertia
8. T 9. The acceleration of an object is directly proportional to the force acting on it and inversely proportional to its mass.
10. To every action there is an equal and opposite reaction.
11. velocity 12. T
13. e 14. a 15. c 16. b 17. d 18. f

Chapter 3
1. T 2. B – elliptical 3. A – faster
4. The straight line joining a planet with the sun sweeps out equal areas in equal intervals of time.
5. T 6. B – Kepler
7. F – his father had died and his mother was poor 8. T
9. A – 3,600 times weaker (60^2 = 3,600) 10. F – to all objects
11. B 12. product, square
13. F – Scientists believe they have found about 100 planets around distant stars.

Chapter 4
1. force 2. A – Archimedes
3. A – effort 4. B – a lever
5. F – at either end or anywhere in between
6. B – reduced
7. M.A. = 9. Mechanical advantage = ramp length/ramp height = run/rise = 9 miles/1 mile = 9

8. C – a wheel and axle 9. T
10. F – it is less
11. B – 18 wheeler truck 12. B – 100

Chapter 5
1. F – only since the 1800s
2. B – energy 3. T 4. D – work
5. energy 6. D – work
7. heat 8. F – The desk must move for work to be done. 9. B – power
10. C – horsepower and watt
11. A – kinetic 12. T
13. F – it becomes four times as great
14. B – doubling its velocity
15. B – potential energy 16. A – heat

Chapter 6
1. A – energy 2. temperature
3. B – water 4. B – expand
5. C – mercury
6. F – They can measure higher temperatures with electrical conductivity and color of light emitted by glowing substance.
7. C – Daniel Fahrenheit
8. A – higher 9. T 10. A – kinetic
11. A – conduction 12. A – copper
13. A – poorly 14. B – convection
15. T 16. T 17. B – greatly different
18. T
19. 0.058 or about six percent. Efficiency = $(T_1 - T_2)/T_1$ = (291 K – 274 K)/(291 K) = 17/291 = 0.058 or less than six percent

Chapter 7
1. F – Because it will snap back to its original shape.
2. T 3. force . 4. B – reduces
5. A – height 6. T 7. C – volume
8. B – decrease 9. B – square root
10. b 11. d 12. a 13. c

Chapter 8
1. T 2. D – wavelength
3. A – frequency 4. B – velocity
5. wavelength 6. T 7. C – pitch
8. A – amplitude 9. A – high
10. F – Both travel at the same speed.
11. tension 12. B – lowest
13. A – acoustics 14. A – better
15. B – twice 16. B – decibels
17. T 18. quality 19. A – same speed
20. A – toward

Chapter 9
1. b 2. c 3. f 4. d 5. g 6. e 7. h 8. a
9. T 10. blue 11. A – reflection
12. B – virtual 13. B – mirror
14. A – convex 15. B – slower

16. A – refraction
17. F – color

Chapter 10
1. T 2. A – electron 3. T 4. charge
5. A – electrostatic
6. B – nonconductor 7. T
8. F – used in golf carts and hybrid cars
9. D – voltage
10. current = voltage/resistance, or in words: current is directly proportional to voltage and inversely proportional to resistance.
11. C – resistance 12. voltage

Chapter 11
1. F – Understanding of magnetism was filled with misinformation.
2. F – It is drawn toward the north magnetic pole of the earth.
3. F – Magnetic north is 1,100 miles from geographic north.
4. B – gravity 5. T 6. T 7. C – iron
8. B – repel 9. T 10. T 11. B – steel
12. A – lost 13. T
14. A – can be turned on and off
15. T 16. D – all of the above

Chapter 12
1. C – James Clerk Maxwell
2. C – the same 3. D – Rudolf Hertz
4. F – FM waves are too short to reflect
5. A – AM 6. C – modulation
7. 3–blue visible light; 1–AM radio waves; 4–x-rays; 2–infrared light
8. D – the second scientific revolution
9. F – color of the light (frequency)
10. T 11. C - photoelectric effect
12. F - mass and velocity 13. T
14. F - Compton effect demonstrates particle nature of light, too

Chapter 13
1. A – electron 2. B – neutron
3. B – a proton 4. A – fission
5. T 6. C – neutrons
7. D – Lise Meiter 8. T
9. D – slow neutrons 10. A – less
11. F – about 20 percent
12. F – Cold fusion is an unsolved problem.

Chapter 14
1. A – far less 2. F – its frequency
3. A – more 4. T 5. A – an electron
6. T 7. A – fundamental frequency
8. B – an electron 9. T
10. velocity 11. a 12. d 13. b 14. c

Index

NEW Parent Lesson Planners Available

INTRO TO OCEANOGRAPHY & ECOLOGY
Parent Lesson Planner (PLP)

INTRO TO METEOROLOGY & ASTRONOMY
Parent Lesson Planner (PLP)

INTRO TO ARCHAEOLOGY & GEOLOGY
Parent Lesson Planner (PLP)

INTRO TO SPELEOLOGY & PALEONTOLOGY
Parent Lesson Planner (PLP)

SURVEY OF SCIENCE SPECIALTIES
Parent Lesson Planner (PLP)

From the Center of the Sun to the Edge of God's Universe

Think you know all there is to know about our solar system? You might be surprised!

Master Books is excited to announce the latest masterpiece in the extremely popular *Exploring Series, The World of Astronomy*. Over 150,000 copies of the *Exploring Series* have been sold to date, and this new addition is sure to increase that number significantly!

- Discover how to find constellations like the Royal Family group or those near Orion the Hunter from season to season throughout the year.
- How to use the Sea of Crises as your guidepost for further explorations on the moon's surface
- Investigate deep sky wonders, extra solar planets, and beyond as God's creation comes alive!

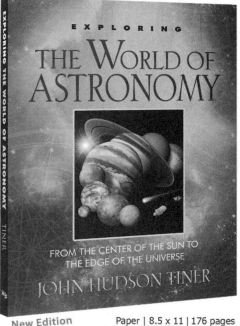

New Edition

Paper | 8.5 x 11 | 176 pages
978-0-89051-787-1 **$14.99**

The book includes discussion ideas, questions, and research opportunities to help expand this great resource on observational astronomy.

Order your copy today to begin *Exploring the World of Astronomy!*

nlpg.com/worldofastronomy

The World of Biology
978-0-89051-552-5
$13.99

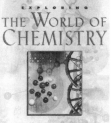

The World of Chemistry
978-0-89051-295-1
$13.99

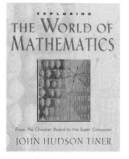

The World of Mathematics
978-0-89051-412-2
$13.99

The History of Medicine
978-0-89051-248-7
$13.99

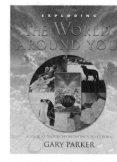

The World Around You
978-0-89051-377-4
$13.99

Planet Earth
978-0-89051-178-7
$13.99

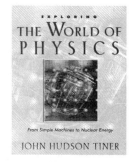

The World of Physics
978-0-89051-466-5
$13.99

nlpg.com/scholarship